MW00413813

PRAISE FOR
RAISING AN ARMY OF
HELAMAN'S WARRIORS

"Today's missionaries are entering the mission field younger than in previous generations. The time and energy required to prepare them adequately for the rigors of the mission field has been compressed. *Raising an Army of Helaman's Warriors* provides parents and Church leaders with some of the tools and resources needed to prepare a cadre of strong and valiant missionaries. Mark and Kevin draw heavily from the scriptures and teachings of Latter-day prophets to support their ideas and counsel. If families will study the scriptures around their kitchen tables, discuss the principles in *Preach My Gospel*, and read and apply the principles in this book, their children will be strongly prepared for missionary service. I can recommend this book to any family that is preparing to send a son or daughter into the mission field."

—**JOSEPH B. WIRTHLIN JR.**, president of the New York Utica Mission, July 2012–July 2015

"With more of our youth leaving for missions, and at an earlier age, it is critical that we pay close attention to helping them better prepare for the rigors of missionary life. As has been said, there is a great difference in a missionary prepared and a missionary who is simply there. In their book, Mark Ogletree and Kevin Hinckley cover a broad range of crucial topics, ranging from personal spiritual preparation to emotional and physical health. They include regular counsel from the First Presidency and the Quorum of Twelve Apostles, as well as personal anecdotes and secular research to help parents and leaders determine how best to prepare their youth. This book has the potential to help us prepare our youth for one of the greatest adventures and sacred opportunities they will experience."

—**MICHAEL A. GOODMAN**, former president of the Thailand Bangkok Mission; BYU professor of Church history and doctrine

"With the lowering of ages for missionaries, the need for parents to create their own MTC is more critical than ever. Ages eighteen for young men and nineteen for young women mean that the actual MTC cannot prepare these young warriors to do battle with the world. It must commence in the home from an early age. This book will help you provide pre-MTC experiences for your youth so that they can hit the ground running."

—**DOUGLAS E. BRINLEY**, former president of the Texas
Dallas Mission; retired BYU religion professor

"*Raising an Army of Helaman's Warriors* contains powerful ideas on teaching and learning in the family. Practical in its approach, this book features subjects like how to discipline children rather than punishing them, working with children to set family rules, and parenting skills that help children learn to be willingly obedient. . . . This book will help equip parents and youth against worldly influences that are only getting crazier with every passing day. More than just missionary preparation, *Raising an Army of Helaman's Warriors* will help parents prepare their children for life!"

—**JOHN P. LIVINGSTONE**, former President of the Michigan Detroit
Mission; BYU professor of Church history and doctrine

"With the historic announcement regarding the change in ages for LDS missionary service, there came an increased responsibility for parents to help prepare their children to enter the mission field. . . . In this book, Mark Ogletree and Kevin Hinckley provide parents, teachers, and youth leaders valuable resources to help us 'raise the bar' in our teaching and training of prospective missionaries. Each chapter is filled with important information, keen insights, and testimony-building inspiration. More than just a pep-talk, *Raising an Army of Helaman's Warriors* provides practical counsel on vital subjects, both temporal and spiritual—conversion, hard work, getting along with others, being guided by the Spirit, and obedience. The chapter on emotional health and resiliency is a must-read. This is a topic parents and leaders must address head-on with our youth today. This book is a treasure trove of practical helps, inspiring counsel, and relevant applications. Thank you, Brothers Ogletree and Hinckley, for providing us—parents, grandparents, teachers, and leaders—with a 'curriculum' for making our homes, quorums, and classes an MPC: Missionary Preparation Center."

—**BRENT L. TOP**, former president of the Illinois Peoria
Mission, 2004–2007; Dean of Religious Education at BYU

RAISING AN ARMY OF
HELAMAN'S
WARRIORS

Happy Father's Day Luke
    raising the bar for missionaries
must also mean raising the bar for the parents
who raise them. The responsibility to teach
the gospel in the Home has never been stronger
than for this generation coming up.
    Thank-goodness you are up to it.
    We know you will be an excellant
        father. We are to proud of you, and
we love you very much.
        love Mom & Dad

RAISING AN ARMY OF

HELAMAN'S

WARRIORS

A GUIDE FOR PARENTS TO PREPARE THE GREATEST GENERATION OF MISSIONARIES

MARK D. OGLETREE, PH.D.
—AND—
KEVIN A. HINCKLEY, M.ED.

CFI
An Imprint of Cedar Fort, Inc.
Springville, Utah

ISBN 13: 978-1-4621-1561-7

Published by CFI, an imprint of Cedar Fort, Inc.
2373 W. 700 S., Springville, UT 84663
Distributed by Cedar Fort, Inc., www.cedarfort.com

LIBRARY OF CONGRESS CATALOGING-IN-PUBLICATION DATA

Ogletree, Mark, 1962- author.
Raising an army of Helaman's warriors / Mark D. Ogletree, PhD, Kevin A. Hinckley, MA.
    pages cm
Includes bibliographical references.
ISBN 978-1-4621-1561-7 (alk. paper)
1. Parenting--Religious aspects--Church of Jesus Christ of Latter-day Saints. 2. Church of Jesus Christ of Latter-day Saints--Doctrines. I. Hinckley, Kevin, author. II. Title.

BX8643.F3O35 2015
248.8'45088289332--dc23

2014048013

Cover design by Shawnda T. Craig
Cover design © 2015 Lyle Mortimer
Edited and typeset by Kevin Haws

Printed in the United States of America

10 9 8 7 6 5 4 3 2 1

Printed on acid-free paper

DEDICATION

Mark D. Ogletree

To Brittany, Brandon, Bethany, Madison, McKenzie, and Cassidy. Thank you for that everything you reminded me of about my own mission as you faithfully served yours.

Kevin A. Hinckley

This is dedicated to my father, Arlo Hinckley, who willingly served a successful mission after returning from World War II. He was also newly married and left his bride to live with her parents as he served the Lord. Despite a life-threatening illness, he returned with honor and set an example for his kids and grandkids to follow. Thank you, Dad!

CONTENTS

INTRODUCTION

"Parents, the days are long past when regular, active participation in Church meetings and programs, though essential, can fulfill your sacred responsibility to teach your children to live moral, righteous lives and walk uprightly before the Lord."[1]

—Quentin L. Cook

YEARS AGO IN a priesthood session of general conference, Elder Neal A. Maxwell prophesied that in the last days, "God will also 'hasten' His work (D&C 88:73). He will also 'shorten' the last days 'for the elect's sake'; hence, there will be a compression of events (Matthew 24:22; Joseph Smith—Matthew 1:20)."[2]

It isn't difficult to detect that "compression" of events in the past decade. We have witnessed more wars and rumors of wars, violence, terrorism, civil unrest, economic collapses, natural disasters, and a host of other calamities than at any other time in our world's history. Meanwhile, we have also seen the gospel continue to go forward without interruption. Temples dot the land, the missionary force is larger and stronger than ever, and—due to a fairly recent national election—the Church has received unprecedented exposure.

This "compression" of events continued at the October 2012 general conference as President Thomas S. Monson made this historic announcement:

> I am pleased to announce that effective immediately all worthy and able young men who have graduated from high school or its equivalent, regardless of where they live, will have the option of being recommended for missionary service beginning at the age of 18, instead of age 19. . . .
>
> As we have prayerfully pondered the age at which young men may begin their missionary service, we have also given consideration to the age at which a young woman might serve. Today I am pleased to announce that able, worthy young women who have the desire to serve may be recommended for missionary service beginning at age 19, instead of age 21.[3]

This historical pronouncement was the "shot heard round the world," or at least the shot heard around the Church. Every social media platform, from Facebook to Twitter, was buzzing with activity the moment President Monson made this declaration. Before the opening session was finished, young men were making plans to leave earlier for their missions. Meanwhile, young women who prior to the announcement were not so sure about missionary service were then texting their bishops and asking for interviews. Fathers were evaluating their financial positions, and mothers were panicking as they realized that some of their children would be leaving the nest earlier than they had supposed. The entire Church was bustling with excitement on the morning of Saturday, October 6, 2012.

Between the morning and afternoon sessions on that historic day, Elders Russell M. Nelson, Jeffrey R. Holland, and David F. Evans conducted a press conference. During the course of the press conference, Elder Holland stated,

> To the prospective missionary, male of female: What does this mean for you? First of all it means that God is hastening His work and He needs more and more willing and worthy missionaries to spread the light and the truth and the hope of salvation of the gospel of Jesus Christ to an often dark and fearful world. . . .
>
> You must prepare by personal worthiness and more cleanliness and you must study diligently to know the gospel you will teach. We want you teaching effectively from the first day onward, and that will require preparation which starts long before you get your call to serve.
>
> We ask parents to take a strong hand in this preparation and not expect that it is somehow the responsibility of local Church leaders or

the missionary department of the Church, or MTC, to provide and direct all of that.[4]

Indeed, God is hastening His work. He is preparing the world for His Second Coming by shortening the last days. To do this, more missionaries will be required to spread the gospel message. Did you notice whom Elder Holland appointed to prepare the future missionary force of the Church? He didn't say it would be seminary teachers or youth leaders. The responsibility falls squarely on the shoulders of parents—right where it should be!

The future missionary army of the Church will need to be better prepared, and they must prepare earlier than any previous generation. Many young men can accept mission calls right out of high school and many young women can leave after their first year of college. This younger missionary force must be full of faith, boldness, and hope; their testimonies will need to be rock solid to be powerful teachers of the gospel. And they must learn these skills from their parents. Parents in the Church will now need to transform their homes into a missionary training center, or better yet a *missionary preparation center.*

RAISING THE BAR

What the Church and the world need is the greatest generation of missionaries to prepare this earth for the return of the Savior. We need missionaries who have been trained to teach and who are qualified to testify of the realities of the gospel. Our youth need to be familiar with the workings of the Holy Ghost and confident enough to identify that Spirit to the investigators they will teach. The days of sending missionaries into the field to shape up, gain testimonies, or be reactivated are through. Today's missionaries must enter the field armed with skills and traits that they learned primarily in their homes.

Because parents have the prime responsibility of teaching their sons and daughters the gospel of Jesus Christ, raising the bar for our future missionaries means raising the bar for parents too! To expect more from our youth will require more from us. Remember that Helaman's two thousand stripling warriors were faithful because "they had been taught to keep the commandments of God and to walk uprightly before him" (Alma 53:21). That instruction came in their parents.

Now more than any other time in our Church's history, we need mothers and fathers who can teach and testify, who can help get the gospel of Jesus Christ deep into the hearts of their children. We need parents who can teach their children about the Restoration, the Atonement, and the Resurrection. Mothers and fathers must instruct their children in principles of obedience, honesty, scripture study, and prayer.

Future missionaries also need to learn how to work hard. Too many parents of the present generation have allowed their youth to slide under the radar when it comes to hard work. Many in our prospective missionary force likely have never worked a fifteen-hour day, walked twenty miles to an appointment, biked from one town to the next, or climbed up and down building staircases several times daily. If missionaries want to be successful, they must be in top physical condition with a strong work ethic. The Church doesn't need missionaries who simply take up space, or worse cause problems for their mission presidents. Of course, our future cadre of missionaries also needs to be familiar with *Preach My Gospel* and *Come, Follow Me.* Both of these programs are the heart and soul of learning to become gospel teachers. Our missionaries must know the gospel, but they must also be able to convey its messages in powerful, strong, and simple ways.

Some may ask what qualifications we have to write a book on preparing young men and women for missionary service. Perhaps our greatest qualification is that we care greatly about the young people of the Church and we have spent much of our lives working with this wonderful generation. We have never been mission presidents, but we have served missions and love the Lord. Kevin served his mission in Manchester, England. His children have served in France, Guam, and the United States. He has worked in many capacities in the Church with the youth and adults as a bishop. Currently, he has a private counseling practice in Plano, Texas, and has written on many topics concerning the youth of the Church. Mark joined the Church at eighteen and was on a mission a year later in Seattle, Washington. After his mission, he worked at the missionary training center while he was a student at Brigham Young University. Like Kevin, Mark has also served as a bishop, in a number of capacities with the youth, and even as a ward mission leader. His children have served missions in South America, Spain, Costa Rica, Missouri, and Ohio. Mark teaches in the religion department at Brigham Young University and also has a private practice in Orem, Utah.

We have probably learned more as fathers regarding missionary preparation than we have in any of our Church capacities or professional jobs. We want to make it clear that we don't have all of the answers when it comes to missionary preparation, but we do believe there are principles and practices that parents can engage in to help their children serve successfully. These principles and practices have been taught and modeled by our Church leaders.

We are grateful to Cedar Fort Publishing and their willingness to work with us on this project. We are also grateful our wives, Janie and Cindy, and their unfailing support, and for our children—so much of what we have learned about these topics has come from our experiences with them!

SUPPLEMENTAL MATERIALS

1. M. Russell Ballard, "The Greatest Generation of Missionaries," *Ensign*, October 2002.

2. "Gathering of Israel": http://www.lds.org/media-library/video/2011-03-101-gathering-of-israel?lang=eng.

3. "LDS Church Leaders Share More Information on Missionary Age Requirement Change": http://www.lds.org/church/news/church-leaders-share-more-information-on-missionary-age-requirement-change?lang=eng.

4. "Press Conference for New Missionary Service Age Requirements": http://www.youtube.com/watch?v=3Uwe9nz2w8k.

REFERENCES

1. Quentin L. Cook, "Can Ye Feel So Now?" *Ensign*, November 2012, 8.

2. Neal A. Maxwell, "'My Servant Joseph,'" *Ensign*, May 1992.

3. Thomas S. Monson, "Welcome to Conference," *Ensign*, November 2012, 4–5.

4. Jeffrey R. Holland, LDS News Release, Press Conference, October 6, 2012, http://www.mormonnewsroom.org/article/church-lowers-age-requirement-for-missionary-service.

CHAPTER 1
THE PARENTS' ROLE IN
TEACHING THE GOSPEL

"I want to tell you—I want to promise you—you fathers and mothers, if you will [teach your children, they] will grow up with love for the Lord, and the greatest reward you can have in this life, nothing excepted, will be to see your children walk in truth before the Lord."[1]

—Gordon B. Hinckley

MISSIONARIES ARE CALLED to teach, preach, and baptize. No one in this Church can be converted without teaching or learning. Though missionaries will have many duties and activities, teaching the gospel will be their key responsibility and privilege. From *Preach My Gospel*, we know "teaching is central to everything [a missionary does]."[2] Teaching the gospel can be broken up into several categories that missionaries will ultimately master: learning to build rapport with investigators, finding common ground with investigators, teaching the doctrines and principles of the gospel, adjusting the teaching material to meet the needs of investigators, learning to teach by the Spirit and from the scriptures, learning to teach with a companion, learning to ask questions that gauge an investigator's understanding, learning to address and resolve concerns, and helping investigators make commitments.

Though many of these teaching skills will be learned on the job, think of how much more prepared missionaries will be if they can learn some of these skills in their homes, long before they leave on their missions. If prospective missionaries can learn how to be powerful teachers, they will hit the mission field running. Soon after arriving in the mission field, they will begin to make an immediate impact. They won't have to spend the first portion of their mission learning to become strong and powerful teachers; instead, they will simply focus on refining their teaching skills. One of the greatest contributions parents can make as they prepare their children for missions is teaching them how to become powerful gospel teachers.

In Doctrine and Covenants 11:21, the Lord stated, "Seek not to declare my word, but first seek to obtain my word, and then shall your tongue be loosed; then, if you desire, you shall have my Spirit and my word, yea, the power of God unto the convincing of men." The first job of prospective missionaries is to seek first to obtain the word, meaning learn the doctrines and principles of the restored gospel. And who will be the first to teach these future missionaries the gospel? Their parents!

From "The Family: A Proclamation to the World," we are clearly reminded, "Parents have a sacred duty to rear their children in love and righteousness, to provide for their physical and spiritual needs, and to teach them to love and serve one another, observe the commandments of God, and be law-abiding citizens wherever they live. Husbands and wives—mothers and fathers—will be held accountable before God for the discharge of these obligations."[3] In order to carry out these prime responsibilities, parents must become strong and effective gospel teachers themselves. Much of that teaching will come through example. However, parents cannot escape their responsibility to teach the gospel directly to their children from the scriptures and words of the living prophets. Teaching changes lives. Teaching is how we'll lead our children back to the Savior and how they will learn to follow the Spirit in their own lives. Teaching is how parents will prepare the next generation of future missionaries.

THE PRIME DUTY OF PARENTS IS TO TEACH THE GOSPEL

Have you wondered how your children would turn out if you didn't have a ward or stake members to help you teach them? What if they didn't have excellent seminary teachers and youth leaders? Elder A. Theodore Tuttle once asked, "How would you pass the test, parents, if your family was isolated from the Church and *you* had to supply all religious training? Have you become so dependent on others that you do little or nothing at home? Tell me, how much of the *gospel* would your children know, if all they knew is what they had been taught at home? Ponder that. I repeat, how much of the gospel would *your* children know if all they knew is what they had been taught at home?"[4]

Elder Tuttle's question is haunting. How much would our children know if all they had been taught came just from us, their parents? Unfortunately, many parents have slacked in this prime responsibility with the hope—or even expectation—that others like Church leaders and teachers would teach their children the doctrines and principles that they never got around to sharing. Perhaps some parents have felt they were too busy to spend time teaching the gospel to their children, or perhaps felt inadequate to do so.

Nevertheless, the Lord has said the prime responsibility of teaching His children falls on the parents in Zion. In a revelation to the First Presidency of the Church, the Lord declared, "I have commanded you to bring up your children in light and truth" (D&C 93:40). Several verses later, the First Presidency of the Church—then Joseph Smith, Sidney Rigdon, and Frederick G. Williams, along with the First Bishop Newell K. Whitney—were called to repentance for not teaching their children the gospel. The Lord declared, "You have not taught your children light and truth, according to the commandments; and that wicked one hath power, as yet, over you, and this is the cause of your affliction" (D&C 93:42). Indeed, regardless of how busy we are as adults in building the kingdom of God or how significant we believe our Church calling to be, there is nothing more crucial than spending time with our families, building relationships with them, and teaching them the gospel of Jesus Christ. If we fail to teach the gospel to our children, then we have failed as parents and in the trust the Lord extended to us.

Elder Henry B. Eyring taught, "A wise parent would never miss a chance to gather children together to learn of the doctrine of Jesus Christ. Such moments are so rare in comparison with the efforts of the enemy. For every hour the power of doctrine is introduced into a child's life, there may be hundreds of hours of messages and images denying or ignoring the saving truths."[5] Think of the thousands of messages that children encounter each day. There are anti-family messages in television commercials. Movies are filled with violence, sexual promiscuity, and satanic themes. Music is filled with messages that can pull our youth away from the standards of the Church. And to top it all off, there's peer pressure and the secular, worldly theories that teachers adhere to and preach as pure truth. If parents do not teach their children, they will still be taught, one way or another. Unfortunately, the messages they'll be exposed to may lead them away from the Church instead of toward it.

THE RISING GENERATION

In the Book of Mosiah, King Benjamin gathered his people together to supply them with teaching and instruction. From Mosiah 2, we read, "And it came to pass that when they came up to the temple, they pitched their tents round about, every man according to his family. . . . Every man having his tent with the door thereof towards the temple, that thereby they might remain in their tents and hear the words which King Benjamin should speak unto them" (Mosiah 2:5–6).

The imagery of these verses is quite powerful. Are the doors of our figurative family tents facing the temple? Do they also face the prophet and the Brethren? Are our tent doors open to receive instruction or closed? Which way does your family tent face? King Benjamin's sermon appeared to be extremely effective. In Mosiah 5:2, we learn that the people who heard this sermon believed the words of King Benjamin and a mighty change came over them. Consequently, they entered into a covenant to do the Lord's will and keep His commandments (Mosiah 5:5). These people became the children of Christ and they took upon themselves Christ's name (Mosiah 5:7–12).

Unfortunately, many of the young children did not stay true to the covenants they made. Just a few years later, we learn that "there were many of the rising generation that could not understand the words of King Benjamin . . . and they did not believe the tradition of their fathers" (Mosiah 26:1). We further come to know that these young people did not believe what had been taught about the coming of Christ or the resurrection of the dead. The scriptures state that they didn't understand the word of God and that their hearts were hardened, consequently becoming carnal and sinful (Mosiah 26:2–4). It appears that the hearts of this generation were hardened. But why? What happened to these young people who seemed to have such incredible spiritual experiences when they were younger? Why didn't they accept the righteous traditions of their fathers? We really don't know. The scriptures are silent on the subject. Did those children who grew up and became rebellious even enter the covenant in Mosiah 5 or were they too young? Did their parents teach them the gospel? Perhaps these young people were taught the gospel, yet they rejected its teachings.

Regardless of the reason, we know that their hearts became hard, they refused to join the Church, and they rejected the commandments, thereby rejecting the Lord. Lest we have another disaster like this, parents need to be actively involved in teaching the gospel in their homes to their children. President Thomas S. Monson warned, "If we do not have a deep foundation of faith and a solid testimony of truth, we may have difficulty withstanding the harsh storms and icy winds of adversity which inevitably come to each of us."[6] This is why parents must teach their children the gospel of Jesus Christ. These teachings will serve as a shield, insulation, and protection against the evils of the world and the snares of Satan. The doctrines of the gospel *can* and *will* protect our children.

Moreover, President Monson's message can certainly be applied to missionaries. While in the field, missionaries must contend with doubt, persecution, and animosity on almost a daily basis. If they are not properly anchored and tethered to the gospel, their testimonies will waver.

Several years ago, the First Presidency issued a letter that was to be read over the pulpit in all congregations. The letter was directed at reminding parents of their duties and responsibilities as gospel teachers. They said, "We call upon parents to devote their best efforts to the teaching and rearing of their children in gospel principles which will keep them close to the Church. The home is the basis of a righteous life, and no other instrumentality can take its place or fulfill its essential functions in carrying forward this God-given responsibility."[7]

This letter served as a reminder of several things. First, the gospel should be central to our lives, and families should not let other activities, no matter how worthwhile, crowd out living it. Second, parents should devote their *best efforts* to teaching the gospel to their children. Often parents spend several hours preparing to teach a lesson for their ward members. We knew of a high councilor who, by his own admission, used to spend almost his entire Saturday preparing for his high council talk the following day. Of course by the time he approached the podium to deliver his talks, there seemed to be only five minutes left in the meeting! This same priesthood leader said that he never spent more than five minutes preparing lessons for his own children.

How often do parents really give their best teaching efforts to their families? Too often, as parents, we substitute the time we should devote to teaching our children with other pursuits. We might rationalize that our children's primary or Sunday School teacher will set them straight on faith, repentance, and the beauties of the Atonement. We even leave testimony bearing to other members of our ward; we suppose that surely someone will testify of Joseph Smith and the Restoration to our children. We may well spend more hours each week preparing lessons for other children in the ward than we do for our own. It may take several hours to prepare a Sunday School lesson; however, when was the last time you took more than ten minutes to whip up a family home evening lesson? Or when was the last time you spent more time preparing an outline for family scripture study than you did for a class scripture study in the Church? Perhaps we, as parents, are preparing banquet for strangers and their children while leaving only crumbs for our own!

Remember that when Alma the Younger was in the darkest abyss of sin, it wasn't the words of his seminary teacher that came to his mind, but those of his father. And when Enos's soul hungered, it wasn't the teachings from a Young Men's president that entered his heart; instead, it was the spiritual teachings from his father. The stripling warriors did not doubt, and that wasn't because of what they had learned from a primary teacher. It was the words of their mothers that strengthened their faith.

Former Primary General President Coleen K. Menlove reminded parents: "Casual, infrequent family prayers, scripture study, and family home evenings will not be enough to fortify our children. Where will children learn the gospel and standards such as chastity, integrity, and honesty if not at home? These values can be reinforced at church, but parents are the most capable and most effective in teaching them to their children."[8] It is not the job of institutions—including the Church—to teach and raise children. That job primarily belongs to parents. The purpose of the Church, as Sister Menlove taught, is to reinforce what parents are teaching at home.

With the announcement of needing more missionaries, and needing them sooner than later, parents must be willing to raise the bar. Many young men will be leaving on missions immediately after high school, and young women will follow shortly after their first year of college. At a recent general conference, Elder Quentin L. Cook urged parents to be more intentional in their role as teachers. He said,

> Parents, the days are long past when regular, active participation in Church meetings and programs, though essential, can fulfill your sacred responsibility to teach your children to live moral, righteous lives and walk uprightly before the Lord. With President Monson's announcement this morning, it is essential that this be faithfully accomplished in homes which are places of refuge where kindness, forgiveness, truth, and righteousness prevail. Parents must have the courage to filter or monitor Internet access, television, movies, and music. Parents must have the courage to say no, defend truth, and bear powerful testimony.[9]

In Doctrine and Covenants 68:25, the Lord instructs parents: "Inasmuch as parents have children in Zion . . . that teach them not to understand the doctrine of repentance, faith in Christ the Son of the living God, and of baptism and the gift of the Holy Ghost by the laying on of the hands, when eight years old, the sin be upon the heads of the parents."

This passage of scripture reminds parents that they are to teach the first principles and ordinances of the gospel to their children. In the same chapter, parents are also instructed to teach their children to:

- Pray and walk uprightly before the Lord (verse 28)
- Obey the Sabbath day (verse 29)
- Work hard and not be idle (verse 30–31)

For parents who are not sure what to teach children, this is your beginning curriculum. It should keep you busy for at least the first semester. The home is where the soil is most fertile; therefore, the home is the prime teaching ground for families. For your second semester curriculum, consider the Church's new teaching program for youth: *Come, Follow Me.* There are twelve topics that coincide with each month of the year, and parents can teach their children in the home, thereby allowing Church leaders and teachers to be the second witnesses instead of the first. If you need material for another semester, use a talk Elder M. Russell Ballard gave to the parents of the Church. He suggested ten significant doctrines, principles, and practices that parents can teach their children so they can become the greatest generation of missionaries. Here is a brief summary of what Elder Ballard taught:

- Understand the Lord, Jesus Christ, and His Atonement
- Develop a meaningful and prayerful relationship with Heavenly Father
- Study the scriptures and learn the gospel
- Keep the Sabbath day holy
- Work and save money
- Pay a full tithe
- Limit the amount of time our youth spend playing video games and viewing media
- Learn to accept responsibility for decisions and keep the commandments
- Learn not to waste time and keep priorities straight
- Recognize the promptings from the Holy Ghost and seek the Spirit[10]

In the divine order of teaching, parents are to instruct their children in gospel principles. Church is where those values and teachings are reinforced—not the other way around! Families are not the safety net to catch those things that are not mentioned in church. The family is the front line of teaching!

Parents can teach the gospel to inspire, train, and even disciple their children. One father related that he had a teenage son in his family who was somewhat contentious. This particular son always seemed to be "mixing it up" with one of his siblings. The father related that this behavior continued for years. Each time it occurred, his parents reprimanded the son as they imposed different forms of punishment. But nothing seemed to work, and the changes in the young man's life never seemed to last more than an hour or two.

Then one day, the father became inspired. After his son caused a huge problem in the family, the father brought the son into his study. Together, they read Ephesians 4:26–32. The father testified to his son that the Lord expected every member of the family not to contend with one other, but rather to be kind and tenderhearted. The two of them then read 3 Nephi 11:29, and the father testified to his son that contention comes from Satan, not from God. When people contend with family members, they are under Satan's influence. The father asked his son what side of the line he wanted to be on: the Lord's side or Satan's. The answer, of course, from the son was that he wanted to be on the Lord's side. The father then testified to his son of the truthfulness of the scriptures they had read and told his son that he loved him, and that the Lord expected more of him, as well as his parents. The father then reassured his son that the Lord would help him overcome his problems.

We wish we could tell you that there was never a cross word uttered in that home from that day forward. But the son didn't change overnight, but gradually he did begin to change. The father continued the practice of teaching his son from the scriptures. The son felt the Spirit during their conversations, and the father felt a love for his son that he had not experienced in a while. In a short amount of time, the son stopped terrorizing his siblings. The father reported that even though the results were not immediate, disciplining his son and teaching him from the scriptures felt right, and he felt for the first time that the Lord was with him as he taught his son.

When our children ask us difficult questions—whether they be doctrinal or practical—we can teach them from the words of the living prophets and the scriptures. For example, when a teenage daughter asks why she can't date at fourteen or why she can't steady date when she is sixteen, instead of saying, "Because that's the rule," or, "The prophet said so," parents can teach their children prophetic truth and testify to them. For example, if there is an issue with the dating standards, parents can read with their children from *For the*

Strength of Youth and testify of those principles. Or when a child has an issue with one of the commandments such as tithing or keeping the Sabbath day holy, scriptures can be read and proper explanations can be given—complete with testimonies. Parents would do well to treat their children as if they were investigating the Church and help them understand the principles of the gospel, just like they would for a nonmember.

YOUTH AS TEACHERS

In order to prepare our youth to be powerful missionaries, they must do more than simply learn the gospel. They must also learn to teach it! The person who prepares a talk for sacrament meeting benefits more than those who hear it, and the teacher who instructs his or her class always gains much more than the students. Knowing these principles are true, why don't we have our children teach the gospel more often than we do? Believe it or not, sometimes it's the "lazy parent" who actually does all the work; it's the lazy parent who always does what is most easy and convenient. For example, a father could teach his son how to mow the lawn and then deal with the yard not looking as perfect as it once did, or he could just mow the lawn while his son sits inside and plays video games. Likewise, a mother could take an hour and teach one of her children how to prepare and teach a family home evening lesson, or she could take the easy way out and whip up a lesson on her own in ten minutes. Meanwhile, her child is playing on his or her cell phone or watching TV while the mother benefits from preparing the lesson. Do we dare ask which of these options will prepare our children best for missionary service?

In Doctrine and Covenants 88:77, the Lord taught, "I give unto you a commandment that you shall teach one another the doctrine of the kingdom." In a family, everyone should be a teacher, children included. The benefits to this are laid out in the following verse: "Teach ye diligently and my grace shall attend you, that you may be instructed more perfectly in theory, in principle, in doctrine, in the law of the gospel, in all things that pertain unto the kingdom of God, that are expedient for you to understand" (D&C 88:78). In other words, as our children teach the gospel, the Lord's grace shall attend them and they will learn more deeply the doctrines of the kingdom—as they teach! The Holy Ghost also comes in the form of "grace." Our children can learn that as they teach from the scriptures, the Holy Ghost will direct their words.

Participation leads to conversion. It's that simple. If we want our youth to become truly converted, they need to be involved. Therefore, if our aim is to have our children deeply converted to the gospel, they should on a regular basis teach family home evening lessons, direct scripture study, and give a talk or spiritual message in family council. The more our children explain the gospel to others, the deeper it will sink into their hearts. Family discussions centered on gospel topics are a great way to place the truth close to the heart of our youth. As the gospel is discussed, children have an opportunity to ask questions and ponder answers.

People learn best when they take on the role of teacher. As children share gospel principles with their families, they will be more motivated to live what they are teaching. Besides that, such sharing of the gospel helps bring families closer. Young men and women will be more prepared and successful as missionaries when they have learned and practiced how to look for answers in the scriptures, identify concepts, and apply gospel principles to their lives.

The gospel of Jesus Christ can be a powerful anchor in the lives of your children. As parents, you can set the tone in your home. You can show your children how much the gospel means to you by how you act, how you teach, and how you live your life. Teach by word and deed. It will make a difference to all involved, including yourself!

PRACTICAL APPLICATION

- Parents, how would you do on Elder Tuttle's test? If your family were the only source of instruction for your children, how well would your children know the gospel?
- Discuss as a couple the indirect and direct ways the gospel is taught in your home. How could you as parents become better teachers to your children?
- What kind of variety could you use to teach the gospel to your children? (For example, role-playing, video clips, music, acting out scripture stories, case studies, and so on.)

- As parents, how could you create more opportunities for your children to be involved as gospel teachers in the home?

SUPPLEMENTAL MATERIALS

1. Jeffrey R. Holland, "A Teacher Come from God," *Ensign*, May 1998.

2. Neil L. Andersen, "Tell Me the Stories of Jesus," *Ensign*, May 2010.

3. *Teaching, No Greater Call: A Resource Guide for Gospel Teaching.*

4. Website: "Come Follow Me: Getting Started": https://www.lds.org/youth/learn/train/introduction?lang=eng.

5. Website: "Teaching, No Greater Call," The Mormon Channel, "Teaching in the Home," Part 1, Episode 26, http://www.mormonchannel.org/teaching-no-greater-call/teaching-in-the-home-part-1; Part 2, Episode 27, http://www.mormonchannel.org/teaching-no-greater-call/teaching-in-the-home-part-2.

REFERENCES

1. Gordon B. Hinckley, "Special Visitor Attends Stake Conference," *Church News*, November 16, 2002, 3.

2. *Preach My Gospel: A Guide to Missionary Service* (2004), 175.

3. "The Family: A Proclamation to the World," *Ensign*, November 1995, 102.

4. A. Theodore Tuttle, "Therefore I Was Taught," *Ensign*, November 1979, 27.

5. Henry B. Eyring, "The Power of Teaching Doctrine," *Ensign*, May 1999, 74.

6. Thomas S. Monson, "How Firm a Foundation," *Ensign*, November 2006, 62.

7. "Letter from the First Presidency," *Liahona*, December 1999.

8. Coleen K. Menlove, "A Voice of Gladness for Our Children," *Ensign*, November 2002, 14.

9. Quentin L. Cook, "Can Ye Feel So Now?" *Ensign*, November 2012, 8.

10. M. Russell Ballard, "Raising the Greatest Generation of Missionaries" (presentation, BYU Women's Conference, Provo, Utah, May 2, 2003).

CHAPTER 2
DISCIPLINE OR PUNISHMENT?

"Children must learn *obedience*, and parents must exact obedience from them. Love your children, let them know that you love them; but remember that it is no favor to a child to let him do things he should not do."[1]

—N. Eldon Tanner

IF A MISSIONARY is to be successful, he or she must learn to be obedient. One of the most vital places that a prospective missionary will learn obedience is in the home through the teachings and practices of his or her parents. There are myriad ways that parents can teach their children the principle of obedience. Besides direct teaching and modeling, many parents engage in discipline or punishment to help their children learn obedience.

So what is the difference between punishment and discipline? Punishment is punitive and reactive while discipline is positive, healthy, and proactive. The purpose of punishment is to inflict pain and penalty for an offense whereas the purpose of discipline is to correct, teach, or train. Parents who punish are usually hostile; parents who discipline show love and concern.[2] In essence, punishment destroys relationships and discipline builds, fortifies, and edifies.

Consider the following scenario: Lisa is driving her mother crazy. For most of her life, Lisa was a good student and a joy to live with. But at thirteen, she has become belligerent and angry. Her grades are falling, primarily because she refuses to do her homework. Lisa's mom is frustrated and angry and wants to restrict all of Lisa's out-of-school activities until "she becomes human again!" Her father on the other hand thinks Lisa's mom is overreacting. He advocates letting their daughter "figure things out" and not push her too hard. "Let natural consequences kick in," he says. "She'll understand when she fails and has to go to school this summer."

Decisions about discipline and consequences cause great challenges in parenting. Missionaries capable of hard work are self-disciplined—they hold themselves to schedules and mission rules, resisting urges to take easier roads. They must learn about discipline and consequences at home and that negative behaviors have certain costs whereas positive actions have their own rewards. They do this as they watch their parents.

The approach we take to a child's misbehaviors says a great deal about how we view our role as parents. It also speaks loudly about what we expect. A child understands—in a hurry—what we are telling him or her by the amount and severity of the penalties they receive. No wonder President James E. Faust once declared,

> One of the most difficult parental challenges is to appropriately discipline children. Child rearing is so individualistic. Every child is different and unique. What works with one may not work with another. I do not know who is wise enough to say what discipline is too harsh or what is too lenient except the parents of the children themselves, who love them most. It is a matter of prayerful discernment for the parents. Certainly the overarching and undergirding principle is that the discipline of children must be motivated more by love than by punishment. Brigham Young counseled, "If you are ever called upon to chasten a person, never chasten beyond the balm you have within you to bind up." (In *Journal of Discourses*, 9:124–25.) Direction and discipline are, however, certainly an indispensable part of child rearing.[3]

Consequences in child rearing often come from either punishment or discipline. The idea of punishment is to inflict enough discomfort that a person chooses not to break the rules again. For instance, if a teen chooses to break his or her curfew, the parents respond by taking away his or her cell phone for two weeks.

While true discipline is *not* emotionally charged, punishment is frequently accompanied by uncontrolled emotion and actions. Punishment implies suffering while discipline is about teaching better habits for living. Discipline is time-intensive, requiring parents to be patient teachers. Unfortunately, many parents are not willing to invest the time to teach. Too many of us would rather yell and get it over with.

The main problem with punishment is that it so rarely works. The reasons it doesn't are fourfold:

- The effects of punishment are usually short-lived. Rather than learn the reason for the rule, kids seem to learn better how to *avoid* the punishment.
- Punishment is often administered when a parent is emotionally charged and reacting to a child's behaviors. Consequences meted out emotionally are subjective and rarely match "the crime."
- Children are not involved in establishing the consequences. Punishment is something inflicted upon them by their parents. For this reason, the focus is on the parent instead of on the child's behavior. Again, what children often learn is more *not* getting into trouble rather than learning more functional behaviors.
- Children who are primarily punished have greater difficulty trusting. They become frustrated because they see their restrictions as arbitrary and unfair. No wonder Brigham Young taught, "Parents should govern their children by faith rather than by the rod, leading them kindly by good example into all truth and holiness."[4]

Consider another scenario: Michelle finds that her fifteen-year-old son had lied to her about going out with some friends. Feeling angry and betrayed by this, she responds by yelling, "Young man, you are grounded!" When he asks for how long, Michelle responds, "When I know you're not lying anymore." Her son then walks away, having no idea how to prove to her he wasn't lying. Furthermore, since she wants him to go to church, school, and sports activities, his grounding lasts for a grand total of two days. Later, her son admits he didn't worry too much when she punished him because she always had to alter it later. What he is really saying is that his mom has no credibility with him and there is no real reason to stop lying. The cost of lying here, for him, was a short "yell session" and a day or two inside. To no one's surprise, he would keep on lying.

The idea behind any corrective action is the hope of a long-term benefit. For example, when a child lies and the parents correct him or her, they are hoping that their child will never lie again for the rest of his or her days. Put another way, they are hoping for a long-term change, not merely a temporary one. As Michelle continually discovered, few things are more frustrating than having to deal the same behaviors over and over again.

The art of healthy discipline must be focused on teaching and training children to make healthy choices and curtailing destructive ones. Successful adults have the ability to make decisions by weighing the consequences of their actions, and then moving forward based on the outcome they want. The children of these adults need to learn to discipline themselves in a similar way so as not to repeat poor choices.

For children to learn this basic success formula, they need parents and adult leaders who can help them connect the dots. Young, immature minds need structure, but they also require experience. Remember that from punishment they merely learn to avoid. Sometimes they actually just become better liars. Therefore, often the end result of punishment is children learning to be more careful so they don't get caught. The deviant behavior stays the same.

From discipline, however, children learn to choose more wisely and keep making the better choice. For a child growing up, the world is filled with many things they want, but it is also filled with parents explaining why they can't have a lot of those things. When youth come face to face with a roadblock to their brand of happiness, their initial tendency is to view parents and leaders as the reason they can't have it. Now the parents become the "bad guy."

PARENTS AS MENTORS AND COACHES

For fourteen-year-old Amy, her happiness hinges on being able to date quickly. After all, her friends all date. Even more enticing is that she has boys who want to date her now! Her body is changing. But she has parents who tell her she needs to wait. The problem, as Amy sees it, is not that she can't handle dating. She thinks to herself, *I am fourteen! Don't you trust me?* The problem to her is parents who don't understand how mature she is and how much she wants to go out. In her eyes, the solution is simple: find a way to make them understand (argue, nag, plead, and so on), avoid them and get what she wants without them knowing, or coping with being miserable and dreaming of the day she'll finally be free. This dynamic can set up constant conflict between parents and children. Depending on how "the problem" is solved, someone has won and someone has lost. From Amy's perspective, dating is not the problem; it's her parents.

Successfully moving from punishing to disciplining involves a fundamental shift in how families solve daily problems. In order for children to learn problem-solving skills, they need to be part of the process of becoming disciplined. To do that, they need coaches and mentors who are focused on helping train and prepare them. Companies all over the world bring in outside consultants to help managers see how they could improve their performance. Employees are willing to participate in such training in the hopes of getting fresh perspectives and ideas that they might not have seen before. In much the same way, growing children need someone to train and teach them how to solve life's problems effectively. This is especially true of teens, who struggle with waves of hormones and emotions as they are preparing to enter a world of adult responsibilities. What they need are parents who will mentor and coach them, helping them define what it is they need to be doing.

Youth need to feel that their parents are on their side and are committed to helping them when they need it. In order to accept that, they first need to believe their parents are not the problem. In the example above, Amy struggles with wanting to date at an early age. She sees the problem as revolving around rigid parents who don't trust her. Amy needs to learn not only what she needs to do but also why. Coaching parents can help her see their reasons for waiting, as well as the Lord's timetable. She can also learn how it's completely normal for girls her age to feel impatient, especially when receiving attention from older boys.

Helping her understand the real problem will also assist her in seeing the why and it will help her understand the necessity of future interventions, if needed.

Amy: "Mom, you just don't understand!"

Mom: "I know it feels like that sometimes. We don't always understand the Lord's counsel until later. I remember feeling the same way."

Amy: "It's not fair. I know other Mormon kids who date."

Mom: "I do too. But that's a decision for their family. I'm sure that it makes it a lot harder on you."

Amy: "Yeah, it does! So what am I supposed to do?"

Mom: "That's the real problem, isn't it? Doing the right thing can be really hard sometimes. Let's talk about that. What can you do that would make the waiting a little easier? I'll help however I can."

Helping Amy understand the real problem is key. At least, children need to understand how their parents see the problem, why they have certain rules, and what blessings come from following prophets and parents.

DISCIPLINE

Understanding the problem helps set up the *why* of discipline. Remember, the purpose of punishment is to punish and the purpose of discipline is to teach. The word *discipline* itself comes from the same root word as *disciple*, which is related to teaching and learning. Disciplined adult behavior recognizes that there are consequences, positive and negative, whenever we follow or break the rules.

For example, as adults, if we want the freedom to operate a car, we first must demonstrate to the proper authorities a proper knowledge of traffic rules and signs and that we know there will be certain penalties if we violate them. If we decide to speed—contrary to the rules we agreed to follow—we also understand that we may be subject to fines or suspensions. Because we don't want to pay expensive tickets, we tend to moderate our driving and stay within the established rules.

Recently, Kevin was in the country of Panama. In the bustling port city of Colon, he was surprised to find a complete absence of traffic signals. Consequently, each intersection was a snarled mess of cars and buses all trying to fight their way through. His guide indicated that there had once been a couple of traffic lights installed in the town. Unfortunately, no one obeyed them, so they were removed. Instead, the people now had to deal with daily chaos at each intersection. The Panama locals had to learn the sad lesson that restrictions such as traffic lights actually could give them more freedom than a complete lack of rules and regulations.

Discipline rests on two major keys: agreeing to rules and agreeing to the consequences. Let's start with the first one.

Agreeing to the Rules

One of the best ways to prevent problems in the home and create order is to establish rules. Rules can guide our children's behavior and make the world more predictable and safe for them. The role of a parent changes over the life of the child. When children are young, parents fill the role of a benevolent dictator. A preschooler's perspective is so limited that he or she requires a parent to decide what the rules are. As children age, however, they are increasingly in a place to have more input into what rules are necessary. They also have greater insight into why a particular rule is vital. True, some rules like restrictions on video game playing or curfews may be a constant source of disagreement, but wise parents can still maintain firm rules using the child's input. Rules that are constantly being negotiated or compromised are not rules! Consider the following example:

Josh: "Mom, I want to go with my friends to the mall tonight. Everyone's going."

Mom: "Josh, you know you can't go to the mall on a school night."

Josh: "Mom! I already finished my homework. I'll be home early, I promise."

Mom: "Josh! It's a school night. You need to stay home."

Josh: "It's just kids from school. Please? I won't be late."

Mom: "No means no."

Josh: "You just don't trust me."

Mom: "I do trust you. But you need to stay home."

Josh: "Mom! They already think I'm a stay-at-home nerd."

Mom: "Okay, quit bugging me! Just be home before ten tonight or you won't be allowed to go again."

So just what *are* the rules about going to the mall on school nights? His mom seems to think the rule is no going to the mall on school nights. If asked, this mother would swear to teachers and everyone else that in their family no one goes to the mall on a school night. However, Josh understands what the real rule is, in order to go to the mall on a school night, don't ask too often, get past at least five refusals from his mom, use guilt, and whine enough to break her down.

Like every household, children quickly learn that rules are not what is spoken; rules are what actually occur when parents get tired and worn down. For instance, youth know that some parents always respond with a quick no, regardless of what the question is. Consequently, they learn how to carefully time and phrase a request, knowing that the real rule is, for example, *Dad always says no, but he might say yes if Mom asks instead of me.*

As children mature, in order to help them stop finding ways around rules, there needs to be an agreement between parent and child as to what the rules actually are. Helpful guidelines for these rules include:

- For most families, fewer rules are better than many rules. This sets up an atmosphere of trust and encouragement.
- Rules that are constantly changing are not rules. Set up house rules that have some flexibility in them to reduce conflict such as a child is only allowed to spend an hour on the computer or a child is only allowed on the computer for an hour unless he or she has checked with everyone else in the house and no one else needs to use it.
- Set the rules together. The more input into house rules that children have, the more likely they are to follow said rules.
- Enforce the rules consistently. If rules are not enforced, then there are no rules.
- When rules are kept, there should be consequences for good behavior. When rules are disobeyed, undesirable consequence should also follow. In Doctrine and Covenants 130:20–21, we read, "There is a law, irrevocably decreed in heaven before the foundations of this world, upon which all blessings are predicated—and when we obtain any blessing from God, it is by obedience to that law upon which it is predicated." Or in other words, when laws and rules are kept there should be an

attendant consequence for such behavior. The same principle applies to poor behavior.

- Set a time—such as family home evening—when rules are to be reevaluated if they are always being compromised or circumstances have changed.

Agreeing to the Consequences

A rule is not a rule unless there are consequences. Unfortunately, many parents—in a punishment-based mindset—declare consequences unrelated to behavior and driven by emotion, taking little to none of their children's input. If they are to become problem-solvers, children need a greater sense of control over their lives as they mature. They need to take responsibility for their actions and gradually rely less on their parents. As children grow and develop (if they have been adequately regulate and prepared by their parents), they will be able to regulated and govern themselves. Parents who feel they are doing their children favors by not having any rules or regulations actually do a disservice to their children. Such children grow up at a disadvantage. Research shows that such children as teenagers and adults can't govern themselves. Living within rules and learning to discipline themselves is key to their growth. One LDS family therapist shared the following experience:

> I ask my teenage clients how they believe they should be disciplined when they've done something they shouldn't have. Universally, they will first joke and give a humorous answer, such as: I think I should have to play computer games until my arms fall off! However, when they see I am serious, they will begin to give me more realistic answers to their "punishment." I continue to be impressed at just how reasonable their self-declared discipline is—and how often it is more restrictive than the one their parents decided on.

In a study done by Brigham Young University professors Brent L. Top and Bruce A. Chadwick, they learned that few youth complained about the strictness of their family rules. On the contrary, several youth wrote that they wished their parents would've been stricter and had given them more guidance during their teenage years.[5] Children know when they've done wrong and they expect consequences. That same LDS therapist asked teens, "What kind of discipline do you think would help you remember not to do it again?"

At some point, obviously, they will probably repeat their negative behavior. This gives parents two wonderful moments. First, they are able to calmly and rationally say something along the lines of, "I feel bad you choose to do that. But at least we know what needs to know happen. You chose to do _____ as a consequence." Second, there will be another moment where, after the consequence is over, that a parent can simply ask, "So, do you think that will work in helping you to not repeat the behavior? Or do you need to change it in any way?"

Those moments are wonderful times to discuss the child's behavior, repeatedly praising him or her for making difficult choices. It also is a time for the child to perhaps examine why he or she behaves in whatever way in the first place. Remember, all behavior has purpose and reason. Children tell their parents more with their behavior than they do with their words. In this kind of discussion, if children can begin to see themselves in that light, they might also be able to better understand their own behavior.

DISCIPLINE AND CONVERSION

When parents learn to discipline in Christlike ways, children respond positively. Often, well-meaning parents harm or even destroy their relationships with their children because of harsh, punitive measures. Unfortunately, every time a parent disciplines in anger, a metaphorical wall is created between them and their children. Each time there is yelling, physical punishment, and put-downs, another brick is placed on the wall. Over time, this wall becomes too thick for anything to get through. By the time some children reach adolescence, they cannot stand their parents. Frustrated mothers and fathers are quick to say of their teen, "They never talk to me." Could one reason be that the wall is too high and thick?

President Joseph F. Smith taught parents how to govern themselves: "Use no lash and no violence, but . . . approach [children] with reason, with persuasion and love unfeigned. . . . The man who will be angry at his boy, and try to correct him while he is in anger, is in the greatest fault. . . . You can only correct your children by love, in kindness, by love unfeigned, by persuasion, and reason."[6]

If parents can discipline their children and preserve a positive relationship with them, such will be highly successful parents. With a positive, healthy relationship, parents will be able to teach their children rather than punish them. If parents can teach their children, they can influence them for good. Part of that process is helping the children have a strong desire to come unto the Savior, repent, and be like Christ. Parenting expert Glenn Latham explained,

> Before we can effectively teach our children *what* Christ would teach, we have to teach them *how* Christ would teach. His ministry was characterized by gentleness, love, patience, persuasion, charity, and long-suffering (see Moroni 7:43–47). Furthermore, He was not easily provoked. We must literally be as Christ (see 3 Nephi 27:27). When we teach that way, we are safe to be with. We are attractive to our children. Our words are believed, our actions are emulated, and our values tend to become their values. They begin to identify with us.[7]

Effective missionaries are disciplined missionaries. They do not require someone constantly standing over them, forcing them to do the right thing. That ability to be self-directing has to begin early in life. They must learn it as they are shaped by daily experiences growing up. They need to internalize it as they experience it at home and see the value of it in their own successes—and especially in their mistakes. Elder Dennis B. Neuenschwander taught,

> Mission rules are important in the same way commandments are important. We all need to keep them, understanding that they give us strength, direction, and limits. The smart missionary will learn the intent of the rules and make them work for him. Your mission is a time of discipline and single-minded focus. You will be required to go without some things common to your current lifestyle: music, TV, videos, novels, even girls. There is nothing wrong with any of these things . . . but then again, there is nothing wrong with food either, unless you are fasting, in which case even a teaspoon of water is improper.[8]

Parents who teach their children the blessings that come from obedience and discipline their children instead of punishing them are well on their way to creating honorable, prepared missionaries. The Savior taught, "For all who will have a blessing at my hands shall abide the law which was appointed for that blessing, and the conditions thereof, as were instituted from before the foundation of the world" (D&C 132:5). This promise has always been true; it will be especially true in the lives of the missionaries who serve the Lord.

PRACTICAL APPLICATION

- Study the following scriptures as a family: Mosiah 3:19; Ezekiel 14:10; and 2 Nephi 2:27. Discuss how these verses could be applied to discipline or punishment.
- Ask your children what the difference is between punishment and discipline? Help them understand the difference. How do they feel when they are punished? What about when they are disciplined?
- For family home evening, discuss with your children what a society would look like without rules. How do rules help keep their home and society peaceful and happy?
- In this chapter, there were scenarios with "Amy" and "Lisa." Have your family act out these scenarios with children playing the role of the parent. Have them demonstrate the difference between punishment and discipline.

SUPPLEMENTAL MATERIALS

1. G. Hugh Allred, "Rational Approach to Discipline," *Ensign*, April 1971.

2. Layne E. and Jana Squires Flake, "Punishment—or Discipline," *Ensign*, October 1983.

3. James E. Faust, "The Greatest Challenge in the World—Good Parenting," *Ensign*, November 1990.

REFERENCES

1. N. Eldon Tanner, "Obeying the Right Voice," *Ensign*, October 1977.

2. Ideas adapted from Chip Ingram, "Punishment or Discipline," accessed from www.focusonthefamily.com/parenting/effective_biblical_discipline/effective-child-discipline/punishment-versus-discipline.aspx.

3. James E. Faust, "The Greatest Challenge in the World—Good Parenting," *Ensign*, November 1990.

4. Brigham Young, *Journal of Discourses*. 26 vols. London: Latter-day Saints' Book Depot, 1854–86, 12:174.

5. Brent L. Top and Bruce A. Chadwick, "Helping Teens Stay Strong," *Ensign*, March 1999, 27.

6. Joseph F. Smith, *Gospel Doctrine* (Salt Lake City: Deseret Book, 1963), 316–17.

7. Glenn L. Latham, *What's a Parent to Do?* (Salt Lake City: Deseret Book, 1997), 27.

8. Dennis B. Neuenschwander, "To a Missionary Son," *Ensign*, November 1991, 43.

CHAPTER 3
TEACHING CHILDREN OBEDIENCE

"Never repeat a clear command. If you repeat it, the child will always wait for the repetition."[1]

—David O. McKay

ONE OF THE most important lessons that every missionary must learn is obedience. From *Preach My Gospel*, we read,

As a missionary, you are expected to keep the commandments willingly, to obey mission rules, and to follow the counsel of your leaders. Obedience is the first law of heaven. It is an act of faith. You may sometimes be required to do things you do not completely understand. As you obey, you increase in faith, knowledge, wisdom, testimony, protection, and freedom. Strive to be obedient to the Lord, the living prophet, and your mission president.[2]

Such missionaries learn that there is a correlation between exact obedience and the presence of the Spirit. We believe that power, protection, and peace come to missionaries who keep mission rules and obey the commandments.

Parents have a sacred duty to teach their children the law of obedience. How will our future sons or daughters obey a mission president when they've never obeyed—or were never expected to obey—their parents? How will they be able to obey mission rules when they never had rules in their home, or were never obedient to the rules they had?

We live in a culture where the media has dumbed down the role of parents. Children learn through TV and other outlets that they *don't* have to obey teachers, Church leaders, or even parents. In some cases, parents have contributed to that disobedience. For example, a bishop shared with us that he was meeting with his ward members for tithing settlement on a Sunday afternoon and was feeling quite tired, hungry, and thirsty. He had been at the church for about seven hours and was simply exhausted. When the next family walked in for their meeting, the bishop politely asked one of the children of the family if he wouldn't mind taking the empty cup to the drinking fountain and filling it with water. The eight-year-old boy said, "No, I'm not going to do that. Go get it yourself." The young boy not only said no to an adult, but to his own bishop who asked him in a nice way.

As parents, what would you have done in this situation? Would you have stopped the meeting right there and taught your child obedience and respect to Church leaders? Would you have grabbed this kid by the ear and pulled him out of the office to set him straight? Would you apologize to the bishop and made this a point of discussion in the car or back home?

What actually happened was the parents laughed and thought their son was really cute and funny. For the most part, they ignored the situation and went on to the next topic. Perhaps they dealt with their son and his disrespectful attitude once they arrived home.

We would have handled this situation differently if this had happened in our families. Mark's style would have been to handle it right there on the spot—the son would have been expected to apologize to his bishop and get him the drink. Then when they got home, there would have been a "Come to Jesus" meeting. Kevin's style would have been a bit calmer in the moment, but once the family arrived home, the child would've been taught some serious lessons and would've been at the bishop's home that night making things right. Unfortunately, some parents today think that everything that their children do is cute and funny—even when it's actually incredibly disrespectful. Poor parenting simply contributes to disrespectful and disobedient children.

HOW MANY TIMES?

As parents, how often have you heard yourself say something like, "How many times have I told you to _____?" Or, "I'm going to count to three and you had better be over here!" Or possibly, "This is the last time that I am going to ask you!" In trying to be nice and keep the peace, many parents buy into the mistaken belief that they need to ask their children multiple times to do things. Children on the other hand learn from this that they really don't need to mind their parents until they have asked three or four times or are beginning to yell and scream.

On one occasion, President David O. McKay was riding on a train to a conference assignment in May 1929. He wrote his wife, Emma Ray, a letter home. Among other things, the letter contained this wise observation:

> There is a lively two-year-old boy here in the car, and a mother who is constantly, constantly, constantly saying, "Donald!" "Donald, don't do that!" "Donald, dear, come here!" etc., etc. And Donald does "that," and Donald doesn't come here, and so another future American citizen gets his first lessons in disregard for law and order. I am so glad I have a loving wife who is also a wise mother, and I love her because she is both and more.[3]

The following example will demonstrate how President McKay lived this principle of first-time obedience. He was riding with his family in their surrey to Huntsville, Utah. His sons, David Lawrence and Llewellyn, were riding in the back seat. As is common with preadolescent teens, David Lawrence and Llewellyn began scuffling and horsing around. In a kind and loving way, President McKay asked David Lawrence to stop. Nevertheless, David Lawrence continued to harass and tease his brother. At that point, President McKay stopped the carriage and requested his noncompliant son to exit the carriage. Years later, David Lawrence reflected,

> I can still remember walking up the hill, seeing the team and surrey going along, getting farther away by the minute. I was old enough to have walked the rest of the way and was certainly in no danger on the country roads of those times; but Father let me walk just far enough to contemplate the lesson in sufficient leisure, then stopped

and waited for me. I was a much-chastened boy when I climbed back into the surrey. There was no more teasing and quarreling.[4]

In too many of today's families, parents don't follow the philosophy of President McKay. Instead, parents ask their children two or three times to complete a task before it gets done, with some of jobs never getting completed. A child may say they are going to do the dishes and then not respond at all to his or her parent's request, even after being asked multiple times. The next morning, the sink may still be full of dishes. Why is this pattern such a common issue in contemporary homes? *This is not a child problem. It's a parenting problem!* Some mothers have conditioned their children not to obey until they count to three or five; some fathers have taught their teenagers not to respond until he is howling and twitching like a crazed wolf!

THE DOCTRINE OF OBEDIENCE

Obedience is one of the most important lessons that missionaries can learn early in their lives. If missionaries obey, they will have the Spirit for guidance and direction. If missionaries choose not to be obedient, they can't claim the blessings of safety, protection, and peace.

One of our children shared the following experience, which was told by his mission president in a zone conference. While at a mission president's conference in Central America, one of the mission presidents received a phone call, informing him that two of his sister missionaries had been abducted. The mission president decided that one of the first things he should do—besides pray—was go and share this news with member of the Quorum of the Seventy who was there conducting the training. The member of the Seventy viewed this as a grave situation. The Seventy member, whom we will keep anonymous, said to the mission president, "President, tell me, are these sisters exactly obedient?" The mission president paused for a moment, thought about the sisters, and replied, "Yes, those sisters are exactly obedient." At that moment, the Seventy member's demeanor changed to one of peace and assurance. He said to the mission president, "Then everything will be okay. The sisters will be all right." Shortly after, the sisters were found with a few bumps and bruises, but they were relatively unharmed. The abductors were taken to prison.[5]

Obedience is a key gospel principle for all members of the Church, not just missionaries. Obedience is considered the first law of heaven. There will be no disobedient people in the celestial kingdom. Joseph Smith once commented, "I made this my rule: 'When the Lord commands, do it.'"[6] As we are obedient to gospel principles and live clean, wholesome lives, a shield of armor is built around us that provides safety and protection. Obedience to the Lord's commandments protects us from temptation, sin, and everyday hardships.

Elder L. Tom Perry promised, "The discipline contained in daily obedience and clean living and wholesome lives builds an armor around you of protection and safety from the temptations that beset you as you proceed through mortality."[7] Can you think of any youth who don't need blessings of protection and safety? Are there any future missionaries who don't need the promise of being protected from temptation?

Where will our children learn obedience? Perhaps in Primary or Sunday School? Maybe they will learn obedience in the MTC? Obviously these are great places of learning. But again, in these settings, wise teachers merely reinforce teachings that should be taking place at home. The laboratory of gospel learning is the home. It is the duty of parents to teach their children obedience. In fact, parents should *expect* their children to be obedient the first time they are asked to do something.

EXPECTING OBEDIENCE

If parents do not teach or expect their children to be obedient, how will they learn later in their lives to respect and obey other authority figures such as their bishops or their bosses? When their mission presidents ask them to serve in the most difficult area of the mission, how will they do it? How will they be obedient to the many rules and standards in their missions? How will they learn to follow the prophet? And perhaps most important, how will they ever follow the quiet whisperings of the Spirit if their parents have not taught them to be obedient? We promise you that your children will never learn these lessons unless they are taught by you at home.

Often, parents assume that their disobedient child will one day simply "get it" and be faithful and obedient until the day she or he dies.

Unfortunately, it doesn't work that way. Children do not wake up after years of disobedience and suddenly become fully compliant. Parents must teach obedience and expect it! It will take courage, patience, and time, but in the end children will learn the first law of heaven.

Though there are many ways to teach children obedience, consider this counsel from Dr. Kevin Leman:

> If you want your child to take you seriously, say your words once. Only once. If you say it more than once, you're implying, "I think you're so stupid that you're not going to get it the first time, so let me tell you again." Is that respectful of your child?
>
> Once you've said it, turn your back. Expect your words to be heeded. There's no peeking over your shoulder to see if the child is doing what you say. There's no backtalk, no argument. You've said your words calmly, and they're over.
>
> Then you walk away and get busy doing something else.
>
> Will your children be mad? Shocked? Confused? Will you have a few days of hassle? Oh yes![8]

Yes, there may be a few days of bedlam (unless you started when they were young), but your children will learn that you expect prompt obedience. Some parents may say, "This sounds great in theory, but what do I do when my child doesn't obey?" We hope you will be realistic here. There's probably a ninety-nine percent chance that your children will *not* catch onto this overnight. Many parents have been letting their children get away with disobedience for years now. Not obeying promptly could be part of family culture. However, they will catch on, especially when they see and feel your obedience to and love for the Lord. Make sure you keep the relationship intact. Don't destroy your children's lives over this concept. Simply balance your relationship and the need for obedience. Don't forget to bear testimony of the value of obedience—to prophets, Church leaders, and the Holy Ghost. As you do so, the Holy Ghost will penetrate their ears and their hearts. Then real conversion can occur!

HOW TO TEACH OBEDIENCE

If there has not been a prevalent spirit of obedience in your home, you can change that. It will take work and effort, but it can happen.

Help your children understand that the way things have been done in the past hasn't necessarily been the right way. In a spirit of kindness, explain to them in a family home evening or family council that you two would like to see some changes in your home. If parents really want to have fun, they can open the Bible Dictionary and read the definition of "repentance." They will learn that repentance involves "a change of mind . . . [meaning] a fresh view about God, about oneself, and about the world." Let your children know that, as parents, you are going to help them have a fresh view on obedience. Teach the principle of obedience and apply it to rules, laws, and commandments. Help your children understand that a culture or society without rules leads to chaos.

If you are not sure where exactly to look in the scriptures, begin in the Topical Guide and search the words *obedience* and *commandments*. You will see that there are many scriptures teaching and reinforcing this principle. Recall that the entire book of First Nephi is saturated with messages of obedience (and disobedience). Other passages include Doctrine and Covenants 82:10; 130:21–22; Moses 5:5; Abraham 3:25; Ephesians 6:1–4; and Acts 5:29. Another great resource is *Preach My Gospel*, specifically page 122. Also, the September curriculum for *Come, Follow Me* is on keeping the commandments. There are some great lessons in this section that will bless our children now and prepare them as future missionaries.

Once you teach your children the principle of obedience, it would be wise to let your children teach it too. Remember that real conversion comes from participation. It's not a bad idea to let your children teach and prepare lessons on obedience. Moreover, if they want to become converted to a principle, they must be invited to live it. You can invite them to practice living a certain gospel principle or to focus on keeping a specific commandment and discuss how they feel after doing so for a period of time.

After you teach your children the principle of obedience, testify of its value and importance in your own life. Surely you've learned it along the way throughout your experiences. If you had the opportunity to serve a mission, there are probably many lessons of obedience you learned that could be passed on to your children. Encourage children to share their feelings about obedience as well. Then explain to them that from this time forth, you expect them to be promptly obedient—not when it's convenient for them or when they get around to it, but when you invite them.

You will want to make sure that your children have an arena to practice obedience. For instance, if there are no rules, expectations, or chores, they won't have all that much to practice. You can help institute obedience in your home by establishing some familial rules and expectations. We recommend that families don't have tons of rules—three to five rules are plenty. However, we do recommend that everyone understands the rules and the blessings and punishments that come when the rules are obeyed or disobeyed (see D&C 82:10; 130:20–21).

As a parent, make sure you are respectful and Christlike as you invite obedience. When children obey promptly, reward them, praise them, hug them, and let them know how much it means to you. Assure them that prompt obedience will be a great blessing in their lives. When children choose to disobey, you must be willing to let the consequences follow. Your children must know that this is a high priority.

We believe we are living in the day when the Lord provides us with specific instructions through His prophets: counsel for our own safety, security, protection, and peace. When we obey promptly, we will be blessed. If we fail to respond quickly, we will reap the natural consequences of disobedience. How blessed our children will be if they learn from their parents to obey promptly. Obedience strengthens faith. If their faith is strong, children will desire to obey whatever the Lord commands.

We know of a young girl who grew up with loving parents. When she was about seven or eight, she was with her family at their cabin. As the parents were working, this little girl was playing with her sisters and cousins. They were having a fun afternoon swinging on a rope swing. As with most children, after a while they became bored, so to spice things up this little girl decided to try some rope tricks. She tied the rope around her neck to show her friends how she could leap off the log pile and swing with "no hands." Just as she was about to jump, her father, who was working some distance away, saw what was about to happen. He knew that if he ran to her, he would be too late. So, he did the only thing that he could. Calling his daughter by name, he yelled, "Stop!" To this young girl's credit, she had learned to obey her parents, and promptly. She froze in her tracks until her dad could run up, untie the rope from her neck, and explain the magnitude of the situation. As a young child, she had no idea that she was about to hang herself in front of her sister and cousins.

Now the haunting question: If this had been one of your children, do you believe they would've stopped in their tracks? Would they have listened? Would they have even heard? We believe children need to learn to be obedient to gospel principles, priesthood leaders, and the Spirit. That process begins with obedience to their parents. As we keep the commandments, we know safety, peace, and protection are promised blessings. Disobedience always leads to heartache, missed blessings, lost opportunities, and often misery. Let us teach our children to obey, and to do so promptly! If our children are obedient to the commandments, they will feel the Spirit in their lives and will have peace—which will lead to their conversion. They will also be safe and protected from sin and temptation, and therefore worthy to serve as missionaries.

Obedient missionaries are strong missionaries. They have the right to call down the powers of heaven. Obedient missionaries live with exactness. They can expect miracles as they serve the Lord.

PRACTICAL APPLICATION

- Study the following verses as a family: 1 Nephi 2:3; Mosiah 5:8; Doctrine and Covenants 82:10; 130:20–21; Matthew 7:24–27; and 2 Kings 5:1–14.
- If you don't have family rules, counsel together as a family and identify three to five rules that your family can live by. Make sure children participate in creating the rules. Also identify the consequences for disobeying the rules and the blessings for keeping them.
- For a family home evening, review *The Missionary Handbook*. Search the PDF file for concepts on obedience and discuss missionary rules. *The Missionary Handbook* can be accessed at https://www.lds.org/bc/content/ldsorg/topics/missionary/MissionaryHandbook2006Navigate.pdf?lang=eng.

- In a family council, or perhaps a more informal gathering, have family members share some life lessons they've experienced from obedience and disobedience.

SUPPLEMENTAL MATERIALS

1. Thomas S. Monson, "Obedience Brings Blessings," *Ensign*, May 2013.

2. L. Tom Perry, "Mothers Teaching Children in the Home," *Ensign*, May 2010.

3. David A. Bednar, "Quick to Observe," BYU Devotional, May 10, 2005; http://speeches.byu.edu/?act=viewitem&id=1456.

4. The Mormon Channel, Youth Videos, "The Sting of the Scorpion," http://www.mormonchannel.org/youth-videos?v=1463142025001.

5. *True to the Faith*, "Obedience," 108–9; http://www.lds.org/manual/true-to-the-faith/obedience?lang=eng.

6. LDS Youth Video, "A Secure Anchor," Richard G. Scott, https://www.lds.org/youth/video/a-secure-anchor?lang=eng.

REFERENCES

1. As quoted in David Lawrence McKay, *My Father, David O. McKay* (Salt Lake City: Deseret Book, 1989), 100.

2. *Preach My Gospel: A Guide to Missionary Service* (2004), 122.

3. As quoted in David Lawrence McKay, *My Father, David O. McKay* (Salt Lake City: Deseret Book, 1989), 100.

4. Ibid.

5. Notes in author's possession. From Madison Ogletree. Interview May 14, 2014.

6. Joseph Smith, *History of the Church of Jesus Christ of Latter-day Saints*. Edited by B. H. Roberts. 2nd ed. rev. 7 vols. (Salt Lake

City: The Church of Jesus Christ of Latter-day Saints, 1932–51), 2:170.

7. L. Tom Perry, "Called to Serve," *Ensign*, May 1991, 39.

8. Kevin Leman, *Have a New Kid by Friday: How to Change Your Child's Attitude, Behavior, and Character in 5 Days* (Revell: Grand Rapids, Michigan, 2008), 33.

CHAPTER 4
THE POWER OF THE WORD

"Never has the Church had a more choice group of young people than at present, and Satan is well aware of who they are. He is doing everything in his power to thwart them in their destiny."[1]

—Ezra Taft Benson

BESIDES THE HOLY Ghost, one of the greatest tools a missionary has is knowledge of and familiarity with the scriptures. It's not the responsibility of a missionary to know the scriptures so well that he or she can bash, brawl, and play spiritual head games with investigators. Instead, missionaries are to become familiar with the scriptures so they can teach the honest in heart true principles and doctrines that will change lives. The scriptures bring the Spirit into the discussions. With the scriptures, missionaries can help others find answers to their questions. Moreover, the missionaries gain great power and strength from God's word.

From *Preach My Gospel*, we learn, "Your ability to teach with power from the scriptures comes in large measure from the time you personally spend studying them. As you daily feast upon the word, your ability to teach from the scriptures will improve. In addition, your invitations to study and ponder the scriptures will be more powerful because you are doing the same thing in your life."[2]

The time to become familiar, comfortable, and confident in the scriptures begins long before our youth enter the MTC. They should begin at an early age to read from the scriptures and gain a testimony of their truthfulness. If our youth learn to apply principles from the scriptures to their own lives, they will be able to help investigators do the same.

Without question, in these latter days we have some of the most faithful cadres of young people ever assembled in the history of the Church. These are outstanding youth. Many of them read their scriptures; many have testimonies of the Atonement and the Restoration; and some attend seminary in the wee hours of the morning. They are faithful members. Nevertheless, at the same time, the world has become an increasingly wicked place, and many of our youth have been caught in the swirling rapids of filth surrounding them.

In their daily walks of life, Latter-day Saint youth face such decadence in their classes at school, during their extracurricular activities, and often around their closest friends. With the advent of the Internet, smartphones, and other technology, many well-intending parents have opened the floodgates of corruption as sex, violence, and disrespect ooze from the electronic media into our homes. Make no mistake about it; Satan has engaged himself in an all-out war against the youth. He views the youth of the Church as his prey, thinking that the young and the innocent are no match for his trickery and deceit.

Where should parents turn for answers to such problems? How do we raise righteous youth who are deeply converted to the gospel? Though we don't know all of the answers to such problems, we can feel certain that the gospel of Jesus Christ—and more specifically its doctrines—will insulate our children against the moral diseases of the world and help their conversion be steadfast and immoveable. Working knowledge of the doctrines of the gospel and a solid testimony of the Restoration can inoculate our youth from the fiery darts of the adversary.

How well do your children know the scriptures? Can they find answers to their problems from the sacred text? When their nonmember or less active friends ask them doctrinal questions, can they provide answers from the scriptures? Do they know where they can turn for peace? Our task as parents is to provide learning opportunities so that our children can know the scriptures and apply them to their lives and situations. Discovering the answers to the above questions while they are young will help our young men and women become strong and faithful teachers of the gospel as missionaries.

GETTING BACK TO THE BASICS

Youth don't need elaborate Church programs to keep them on the straight and narrow path and prepare them for becoming valiant missionaries. Moreover, parents do not need to master extravagant techniques to help bring their sons and daughters to the Savior. Perhaps the solutions are simpler than we have previously imagined.

A youth leader back in the late 1980s shared with us the following experience:

> Years ago, after I graduated from Brigham Young University, I took my first job and we relocated to Mesa, Arizona. On the rumor that I was a full-time seminary teacher for the Church, a member of the bishopric tracked me down about two weeks before we moved into our home and called me to be a teacher's quorum advisor in the Young Men's program. It was a great experience. We had a vibrant teacher's quorum with over thirty young men. I soon found out that I was not the only advisor. We actually had five advisors just to perform crowd control during Sunday lessons. While serving in the quorum, we had many great activities. My first summer as a leader, our High Adventure took us to Guaymas, Mexico. There, we had the great occasion to snorkel and scuba dive for a week in the beautiful waters of the Pacific Ocean. The next year, we headed to the Colorado Rockies for a week-long backpacking experience. Both were wonderful adventures, and the boys had an excellent time, as did the leaders.
>
> Meanwhile, where were the Mia Maids? Were they having as much fun at girls' camp? What were they doing? Every year it seemed to be the same thing. They were at Camp Liahona or something like that, participating in service projects, passing off camp requirements, making quilts, baking bread, and bearing their testimonies. The girls would often complain because they never seemed to get to do what the young men were allowed to do. Nevertheless, each year the girls pressed forward to Camp Liahona, making more humanitarian kits, reading their scriptures, and having life-changing experiences. Meanwhile, the young men were jumping off cliffs, lighting each other on fire, and throwing rocks at cars—we called that High Adventure.

As I reflected on the difference between the High Adventure program and girls' camp, I realized that the young women were doing some beneficial things that would prepare them for their future. They were immersed in the Spirit and learning key skills that would serve them well throughout the rest of their lives. At the same time, the young men were in some lagoon in Mexico, torturing jellyfish and sticking their fingers in each other's snorkels. The more I thought about that, the more I realized that the young women might be onto something.

About the same time these young men were exploring the lagoons of Mexico, the Church conducted a study of the Latter-day Saint youth. Though the study focused on the young men of the Church, the principles could certainly apply to young women as well. The objective of the study was to identify child-rearing outcomes that could be measured. How could parents and leaders feel that they were successful in raising their children? The following were identified:

- Ordination to the Melchizedek Priesthood
- Serving a full-time mission
- Receiving the temple endowment
- Marrying in the temple

Conceivably, there are other outcomes that could have been included; however, as Elder Gene R. Cook explained, "Perhaps any parents whose son [or daughter] had accomplished those four gospel outcomes could feel, in some measure, successful as parents. At least they would feel that they had launched their son [or daughter] on the road to eternal life. Perhaps no other gospel outcomes outweigh those identified above."[3]

What factors lead to these outcomes? Incredible Scout activities? High Adventures in the Rockies? What about Camp Liahona? An exceptional Young Women's president? What about that popular seminary or Sunday School teacher? A great bishop? Amazing sacrament meetings? Actually, it wasn't any of these things. What the researchers discovered was extremely simple. The answer was so simple that many had overlooked it. *Personal prayer* and *personal scripture study* were the highest-correlated factors with the outcomes identified. In fact, the association between these two variables and the four identified outcomes was over ninety percent, which is practically unheard of when dealing with human subjects. Put another way, if we want to our youth to be ordained to the Melchizedek Priesthood, receive their endowments in the temple, serve in the mission field, and marry in the temple, then we need to find ways to help them more regularly use and rely on the scriptures and prayer.

The next question was obvious: How do we motivate our children to pray and read the scriptures on their own? Once again, the results were quite simple. What the researchers discovered was that the highest-correlated variables with personal prayer and scripture study were:

- Family prayer
- Family scripture study and family home evening
- Family agreement on values

Elder Cook further explained,

If we want our children to pray, we must show them by example through family prayer. If we want our children to read the scriptures, they need to see the scriptures being read in the family. The factor that has the greatest effect on private religious behavior is family worship, meaning that the family is having regular family prayer, family scripture study, and family home evening.[4]

So, as parents and Church leaders, where should we be spending our time with our youth? Obviously we need to spend less time planning activities and doing things that have little eternal significance. We need to focus our time and attention on getting them reading the scriptures and getting down on their knees. Our youth also need to know how much we as parents love the scriptures and how meaningful prayer is to us.

STUDYING THE SCRIPTURES

If we want our children to be truly converted, to become stalwart missionaries, they must learn the gospel from the scriptures and be able to teach from them too! As they read from sacred writings, the Holy Ghost will testify to them of the truths of the gospel. There is power in the word of God. Most are now familiar with Elder Boyd K. Packer's statement, "True doctrine, understood, changes attitudes and behavior.

The study of the doctrines of the gospel will improve behavior quicker than a study of behavior will improve behavior."[5] The greatest source of doctrine we have is found in the scriptures. The scriptures have the power to change lives. Not only does the doctrine change people, anchoring them to the Savior, but by studying the doctrines of the gospel, their access to the Holy Ghost increases. These are certainly blessings that all could benefit from.

The following is an excerpt from one of the greatest talks never given. That's right, *never* given. It was during the April 1986 general conference and President Ezra Taft Benson simply ran out of time to share this message. Fortunately, it was printed in the *Ensign* along with the other conference talks. Unfortunately, many members of the Church are still unaware of it. Had this talk been delivered, it may well have been received with the same reverence and respect as President Benson's talk on pride and the Book of Mormon.

> I add my voice to these wise and inspired brethren and say to you that one of the most important things you can do as priesthood leaders is to immerse yourselves in the scriptures. Search them diligently. Feast upon the words of Christ. Learn the doctrine. Master the principles that are found therein. There are few other efforts that will bring greater dividends to your calling. There are few other ways to gain greater inspiration as you serve.
>
> But that alone, as valuable as it is, is not enough. You must also bend your efforts and your activities to stimulating meaningful scripture study among the members of the Church. *Often we spend great effort in trying to increase the activity levels in our stakes. We work diligently to raise the percentages of those attending sacrament meetings. We labor to get a higher percentage of our young men on missions. We strive to improve the numbers of those marrying in the temple. All of these are commendable efforts and important to the growth of the kingdom. But when individual members and families immerse themselves in the scriptures regularly and consistently, these other areas of activity will automatically come. Testimonies will increase. Commitment will be strengthened. Families will be fortified. Personal revelation will flow.*[6]

After reading President Benson's message, perhaps we should focus more on the word of God and less on some of the other programs we have often tried to implement. If we want our children to be truly converted, they need to be reading the scriptures. To prepare a cohort of rock-solid, faith-filled missionaries, we need to be teaching our children from the scriptures, and more important, teaching them to be reading the scriptures for themselves. From *Preach My Gospel*, we learn,

> We show our faith by studying, believing, and obeying God's revealed word. We diligently search the scriptures to understand the truth. We feast upon them because they open the door to revelation and show us what we need to do and become. We search the scriptures to learn about Jesus Christ and His gospel. Faith in Jesus Christ is a gift from God and comes through studying and living His word and His gospel. . . . We should study [the scriptures] daily.[7]

Our children will strengthen their testimonies and shore up their faith as they study the scriptures. This will be one of the most significant practices they can engage in as they prepare for missionary service. The likelihood of them being immersed in the scriptures is directly related with their parents' willingness to read and study as well. Parents must pass down to their children their own beliefs, testimonies, and experiences with the scriptures. Do your children know how you feel about the scriptures? Do they know some of your favorite passages? Do they know who your scripture heroes are? Have you shared your testimony of the scriptures with your family? It's not enough to simply tell our children about the scriptures; they must feel what their parents feel. We must convey to our children what the scriptures mean to us.

THE BLESSINGS OF SCRIPTURE USE

Time and space will not permit elaborate explanations as we mention the blessings of scripture use. Instead, we will share teachings from the Brethren that echo our own feelings about the blessings of the scriptures in our lives and in the lives of our children. These are the reasons we want our own children to read the scriptures, and why we as parents should read them as well.

We want our children to come to know the Lord
• President Gordon B. Hinckley

> Brothers and sisters, without reservation I promise you that if you will prayerfully read the Book of Mormon, regardless of how many times you previously have read it, there will come into your hearts an added

measure of the Spirit of the Lord. There will come a strengthened resolution to walk in obedience to his commandments, and there will come a stronger testimony of the living reality of the Son of God.[8]

We want our children to hear the voice of the Lord
* Elder Gene R. Cook

One of the most important things learned in reading the scriptures is how to hear the voice of the Lord *to us*. Instruction comes not only from reading the words; when we prayerfully ponder them, the Lord can speak "between the lines" to us. In other words, He can speak to us about our current problems while we are reading the content of the scriptures. In fact, the very act of reading them (it almost doesn't matter where) seems to open the door to direction from the Lord if we approach our reading humbly. The scriptures are one of the greatest tools we have for communicating with the Lord. Elder Bruce R. McConkie once told me he had received more revelation while reading the scriptures than in any other way. I bear testimony that the same is true for me.[9]

We want our children to feel the power that comes from scripture reading
* Elder Bruce R. McConkie

I think that people who study the scriptures get a dimension to their life that nobody else gets and that can't be gained in any way except by studying the scriptures. There's an increase in faith and a desire to do what's right and a feeling of inspiration and understanding that comes to people who study the gospel—meaning particularly the Standard Works—and who ponder the principles, that can't come in any other way.[10]

We want our children to be able to resist temptation
* President Ezra Taft Benson

There is a power in the [Book of Mormon] which will begin to flow into your lives the moment you begin a serious study of the book. You will find greater power to resist temptation. You will find the power to avoid deception.[11]

We want our children to receive answers to their prayers
* Elder Boyd K. Packer

If your [seminary and institute] students are acquainted with the revelations, there is no question—personal or social or political or occupational—that need go unanswered. Therein is contained the fulness of the everlasting gospel. Therein we find principles of truth that will resolve every confusion and every problem and every dilemma that will face the human family or any individual in it.[12]

We want our children to experience love in our homes
• Marion G. Romney

I feel certain that if, in our homes, parents will read from the Book of Mormon prayerfully and regularly, both by themselves and with their children, the spirit of that great book will come to permeate our homes and all who dwell therein. The spirit of reverence will increase; mutual respect and consideration for each other will grow. The spirit of contention will depart. Parents will counsel their children in greater love and wisdom. Children will be more responsive and submissive to the counsel of their parents. Righteousness will increase. Faith, hope, and charity—the pure love of Christ—will abound in our homes and lives, bringing in their wake peace, joy, and happiness.[13]

WAYS THE SCRIPTURES CAN BE USED IN OUR HOMES

First, as parents, set the example of scripture reading, scripture study, and finding answers to problems in the scriptures. Do not be afraid to let your children catch you with your scriptures open, marking pencil in hand. When children see you reading the word of God, praying, and discussing the scriptures, they will learn how much the scriptures mean to you. They will also see and know for themselves the source of your personal strength.

Second, teach life lessons from the scriptures. Every problem that your children face can be answered in the scriptures. Are your children struggling with their prayers? Maybe the prophet Enos could teach them a thing or two. Does their faith need to be strengthened? Nephi sounds like just what the doctor ordered. Are they experiencing peer pressure? That sounds like what Daniel experienced. Furthermore, teach your children how to apply the scriptures to their lives. What scripture stories inspired you as a youth, young adult, or missionary? Share those with your children, as well as what they mean to you.

Third, don't hesitate to discipline your children from the scriptures. Obviously, you wouldn't want to bark scriptures in their ears when they make mistakes. For example, if a child struggled with dishonesty, reaming them out by shouting, "Wo unto the liar, for he shall be thrust down to hell" (2 Nephi 9:34), would probably not inspire them to improve their behavior or increase their love of the scriptures. However, when the moment is tender and emotions are in check, why not turn to 3 Nephi 11:29 and teach about contention? Do you have a child who is critical and cannot say anything nice about others? Read Ephesians 4:29 and bear your testimony about the importance of kind words and of how our Heavenly Father wants us to speak to each other. Do your children treat each other unkindly? Share with them the teachings of Paul from 1 Corinthians 13, or Moroni 7, and discuss what it means to be charitable and help them pray for the gift of charity.

As you learn to discipline your children from the scriptures, you will feel the Spirit of the Lord with you and will come to understand the wonderful benefits of teaching your children with the Spirit. Your children will feel a greater love for you as you teach them from the scriptures. They will respond to your words, and you will feel like you are walking on the Savior's path as a parent.

Fourth, make time to read the scriptures as a family. We would recommend doing this the same time each day. That way, the family will understand that the scripture routine is as sure as the sun rising each day. Consistency can be a real key to conversion. Elder David A. Bednar related,

> Today if you could ask our adult sons what they remember about family prayer, scripture study, and family home evening, I believe I know how they would answer. They likely would not identify a particular prayer or a specific instance of scripture study or an especially meaningful family home evening lesson as the defining moment in their spiritual development. What they would say they remember is that as a family we were consistent.[14]

However, scripture reading doesn't have to be drudgery. Parents can be creative in their teaching. Ask questions, use media helps and object lessons, role-play, and help your youth apply the scriptures to their personal lives. The *Come, Follow Me* curriculum is packed with videos and supplemental materials that parents can use to make scripture study more relevant.

Fifth, have a scripture that serves as a theme each month in your family. The scripture should center on a topic your family is working on. For example, if the topic is charity, then Moroni 7:45 could be posted throughout the home and cited in family home evening, family council, and scripture study meetings.

Sixth, create a spiritual environment in your home by placing sacred books on tables and scripture-based pictures on the walls. It would be good if there were scriptures that could be found in almost every room of your home. This exposure of the scriptures will peak the reading interests of your children and will also create a reverent spirit in your home.

Seventh, make the scriptures the center of your family by showing their importance to your children. Who will question or doubt your love of God's word if you talk about it when you sit in the house, walk by the way, retire at night, or awake in the morning (see Deuteronomy 6:6–7)? A mother who has a set of scriptures in her car to read as she waits for her children to finish their activities has already preached a sermon without saying a word. A father who is found in the early morning hours reading his scriptures at the kitchen table has done the same.

Eighth, never be afraid to give your children a personalized set of scriptures. When children turn eight, when they begin seminary, when they leave for the mission field, and when they get married are prime times to give such gifts. A set of scriptures with your child's name engraved in them, along with a personal message from parents regarding what these scriptures mean, will be not just a gift but a priceless treasure.

There is power in the word of God. The sooner children discover that, the better off they will be. They will become deeply converted to the gospel. As they serve in the mission field, their time will be spent teaching powerful lessons and quoting scripture instead of trying to determine if they have a testimony or not. As teachers, they will be able to say the right thing at the right moment, thereby helping to bring the gospel to Heavenly Father's children.

PRACTICAL APPLICATION

- Study the following verses as a family: Alma 31:5; 2 Nephi 32:3; Jacob 2:8; 1 Nephi 19:23; 2 Nephi 4:15–16; and 2 Timothy 3:15–17. Discuss the concepts that these scriptures teach.

- If you don't have consistent family scripture study, decide as a family when and how you will incorporate scripture study into your family schedule.
- For a family home evening, read and study chapter 3 in *Preach My Gospel.*
- As a family, select a scripture theme each month or pick a scripture to memorize.
- As parents, regularly incorporate scripture stories into your teaching in the home. Discover how you can apply Deuteronomy 6:6–7.

SUPPLEMENTAL MATERIALS

1. Anne G. Wirthlin, "Teaching Our Children to Love the Scriptures," *Ensign*, May 1998.

2. Julie B. Beck, "My Soul Delighteth in the Scriptures," *Ensign*, May 2004.

3. Lori Fuller, "Scripture Study for Family Strength," *Ensign*, August 2013.

4. "Using Preach My Gospel in Scripture Study," *Ensign*, December 2009.

5. The Mormon Channel, *Gospel Solutions for Families*, "Power of the Scriptures"—Part 1, Episode 40; http://www.mormon channel.org/gospel-solutions-for-families/40-power-of-the-scriptures-part-1; "Power of the Scriptures"—Part 2, Episode 41; http://www.mormonchannel.org/gospel-solutions-for-families/41-power-of-the-scriptures-part-2.

6. *True to the Faith*, "Scriptures," 155–59; http://www.lds.org/manual/true-to-the-faith/scriptures.p1?lang=eng.

7. LDS Youth Website, "How to Build Faith in God through Scripture," D. Todd Christofferson, https://www.lds.org/youth/article/build-faith-in-god-through-scripture?lang=eng.

REFERENCES

1. Ezra Taft Benson, *Teachings of Ezra Taft Benson* (Salt Lake City: Deseret Book, 1988), 562–63.

2. *Preach My Gospel: A Guide to Missionary Service* (2004), 180.

3. Gene R. Cook, *Raising Up a Family unto the Lord* (Salt Lake City: Deseret Book, 1993), 17–18.

4. Ibid., 19.

5. Boyd K. Packer, "Little Children," *Ensign*, November 1986.

6. Ezra Taft Benson, "The Power of the Word," *Ensign*, May 1986, 81; emphasis added.

7. *Preach My Gospel: A Guide to Missionary Service* (2004), 73.

8. Gordon B. Hinckley, "The Power of the Book of Mormon," *Ensign*, June 1988, 6.

9. Gene R. Cook, *Raising Up a Family unto the Lord* (Salt Lake City: Deseret Book, 1993), 109.

10. Bruce R. McConkie, *Church News*, January 24, 1976, 4; as cited in "Teachings of Latter-day Prophets of the Blessings of Scripture Study," *New Testament Class Member Study Guide*,1997, 27–28.

11. Ezra Taft Benson, *The Teachings of Ezra Taft Benson* (Salt Lake City: Bookcraft, 1989), 54.

12. Boyd K. Packer, "Teach the Scriptures," address to religious educators, October 14, 1977, 5; as cited in *Teaching, No Greater Call*, "Lesson 10: The Power of the Word," Part B, 51.

13. Marion G. Romney, "The Book of Mormon," *Ensign*, May 1980, 67.

14. David A. Bednar, "More Diligent and Concerned at Home," *Ensign*, November 2009, 19.

CHAPTER 5
HAVE YE INQUIRED
OF THE LORD?

"Simply stated, testimony—real testimony, born of the Spirit and confirmed by the Holy Ghost—changes lives."[1]

—M. Russell Ballard

I N OCTOBER 1974 then new President Spencer W. Kimball spoke to Church leaders at a regional representatives' seminar. He addressed the General Authorities and regional representatives and gave the charge that the gospel of Jesus Christ should now go to the uttermost parts of the earth. President Kimball said that the time had come to teach the entire world and that we should be praying that doors would open behind iron and bamboo curtains, and every nook and cranny of the earth.

He further explained that this worldwide expansion could not occur if the Church wasn't ready and if we didn't have a missionary force equal to the task. To enlarge the vision of the Church, President Kimball urged every young man who was worthy to serve a mission. He then said, "Far too many young men arrive at the missionary age quite unprepared to go on a mission, and of course they should not be sent. But they should all be prepared."[2] President Kimball then stated,

"I am not asking for more testimony-barren or unworthy missionaries. I am asking that we start earlier and train our missionaries better in every branch and every ward in the world."[3]

We are long past the day when young men go into the mission field to seek testimonies, reform, and become converted. Instead, the Church needs young men and women who are well-prepared and who can teach the gospel the first day they arrive on their missions. They need to be assets to their missions, not liabilities. Now, with missionaries able to serve at an earlier age, young men and women must gain strong testimonies in their youth!

Gaining a testimony of the gospel may be the first crucial step a teenager can personally take toward conversion. The strength of the Lord's Church lies in the personal testimonies of its members. A personal testimony is the foundation of faith, and it's the source of power and strength in the Church. Testimonies of the gospel are what sustain us in times of trial, strengthen us in times of peace, and help guide, direct, and shape our lives into becoming disciples of Jesus Christ. If we want to send powerful young men and women into the mission field, they must have rock-solid testimonies of the gospel.

When compared to teens across America, Latter-day Saint youth are stellar when it comes to testimony. In 2001, a group of researchers from the University of North Carolina at Chapel Hill conducted one of the most comprehensive studies of American youth and religion that has ever been attempted. Their research, known as the *National Study of Youth and Religion*, documented that American youth are much stronger, religiously speaking, than many had supposed. In this landmark study, seventy-one percent of LDS youth reported attending Church at least weekly, compared to forty percent of Catholic teens and forty-four percent of Protestant adolescents. What perhaps is even more impressive is the response to the question, "Would you attend Church if it were totally up to you?" Almost seventy percent of LDS youth responded yes to that query, with forty-seven percent of Protestant youth and forty percent of Catholic teens responding in the same manner.[4]

Though these statistics paint a favorable picture for Latter-day Saint youth, we are aware that many of our youth lack testimonies, which is evident in some of their behaviors and choices. For example, in a meeting of Young Men's leaders recently, a concern was brought up about a young man who rarely attended his meetings. In his defense, another leader piped up and said, "Actually, that young man has a stronger testimony than any of the youth in the entire ward." Really? So that young man has a stronger testimony than the young men who fulfill their Aaronic Priesthood responsibilities weekly without being asked? That young man has a stronger testimony than the youth who attend seminary and read their scriptures daily? We highly doubt that. Why? *Because a testimony drives behavior.*

HAVE YE INQUIRED OF THE LORD?

You may recall in 1 Nephi 15 that Nephi's brothers were contending over the things their father, Lehi, had taught them concerning the natural branches of the olive tree and the Gentiles in 1 Nephi 10. Nephi taught his brothers that the only way such doctrine and teachings could be understood was by asking the Lord for understanding and enlightenment (1 Nephi 15:3). Nephi's exact question to his brothers was, "Have ye inquired of the Lord?" Of course, their response was that they hadn't asked the Lord anything. A closer look at 1 Nephi 15 indicates that they did not even think of asking God about such things because of the "hardness of their hearts" (1 Nephi 15:4; see also 1 Nephi 15:11).

Consequently, Nephi's instructions are applicable to all who are searching for the truth. In 1 Nephi 15:10, Nephi chastens his brothers for not keeping the commandments and having hard hearts. Nephi then instructed them, in verse 11, to soften their hearts, ask the Lord in faith, believe that they shall receive an answer, and keep the command- ments. If Laman and Lemuel would take these steps, then "these things shall be made known unto [them]." This pattern holds true for all of our youth in the latter days. If they will soften their hearts, ask the Lord in faith, believe that they will receive an answer, and keep the commandments, the Lord will reveal answers to them in His time. Moreover, as they humble themselves, they will feel His spirit and receive answers to their prayers (D&C 112:10). Their testimonies will begin to take root.

Inquiring of the Lord means going to the source of truth and light for answers. If our youth want to know that God lives, that Jesus is the Christ, and that Joseph Smith saw them both, they need to go to the source and inquire of the Lord. If they want to know that the Book of Mormon is true, they must ask the "Eternal Father, in the name of Christ," and if they ask "with a sincere heart, with real intent, having faith in Christ," He will manifest the truth unto them, "by the power of the Holy Ghost" (Moroni 10:4).

We must emphasize to our children that the Book of Mormon is the keystone of our religion, our doctrine, and our testimonies. The Church stands or falls based on the truthfulness of the Book of Mormon. Take away the book and we simply do not have a church or a religion.

Furthermore, our youth need to understand that if the Book of Mormon is true, then Joseph Smith has to be a prophet. If Joseph Smith is a true prophet, then everything he taught is true! If everything that Joseph taught is true, then there is a God, and Jesus Christ is our Savior and Redeemer. Also, if the Book of Mormon is true and Joseph Smith is a divinely appointed prophet, then the line of succession continues and Thomas S. Monson is a prophet today—and everything that he teaches us is true. When prophets bear witness of God the Father, Jesus Christ, the Holy Ghost, temple marriage, and eternal families, it's all true. Indeed, everything rises and falls with the Book of Mormon. It all hinges on coming to know that it is a true record. If the Book of Mormon is true, then our youth can gain testimonies that they are in the right place, doing the right thing, at the right time. If the Book of Mormon isn't true, then this Church and its people are the biggest hoax quite possibly ever.

The beauty of that dilemma is individual members can find out for themselves. There is no pressure to conform, there is no brainwashing or coercing—members of this Church can know the truth independently, just as Joseph found out, as well as millions of others!

WHAT IS A TESTIMONY?

A testimony of the gospel comes from the Holy Ghost. A person can come to know the truth through the medium of the Spirit. A testimony comes when we receive pure knowledge from the Holy Ghost; it will anchor us to the Savior and help guide us back to our Heavenly Father. A rock-solid testimony anchors a missionary when he or she is exposed to the storms of lies and half-truths about the gospel, challenges, and various forms of opposition that come.

The foundation of a testimony is built on certain truths. We must have a knowledge that:

- We have a loving Heavenly Father
- Jesus Christ is our Savior and Redeemer
- We can be cleansed from our sins and return back to God because of the Atonement
- Joseph the Prophet helped restore the gospel of Jesus Christ to the earth in the last days
- The Book of Mormon is true and contains the fulness of the gospel
- We have a living prophet today who reveals the Lord's will to us
- The Church of Jesus Christ of Latter-day Saints is the true church upon the earth

Our youth need to understand that a testimony cannot be taken for granted. Testimonies are fragile. Like a garden, a testimony must be constantly nourished, watered, fertilized, and weeded. President Harold B. Lee taught, "A testimony is fragile. It is as hard to hold as a moonbeam. It is something you have to recapture every day of your life."[5] Just because you have a testimony today doesn't guarantee that you'll have one tomorrow. Unless our testimonies are constantly fed, they can fade rather quickly.

Therefore, each of us should be seeking to strengthen our testimonies daily. We need to read the scriptures faithfully, engage in meaningful prayer, seek to serve those around us, and keep the commandments.

HOW TO GAIN A TESTIMONY OF THE GOSPEL

Gaining a testimony is a prime responsibility of our youth. It is on their shoulders—no one can gain a testimony for them. Parents can't give to children their own personal faith, convictions, or spiritual experiences. There can't be a transfusion of belief from parent to child. Each must seek and obtain their own.

Furthermore, a testimony is not likely to develop automatically from attending Church meetings, seminary, or other activities. A testimony takes work and effort. Nothing good comes without effort, persistence, and sacrifice. Elder John A. Widtsoe said the steps that lead to a testimony are desire, prayer, study, and practice.[6] Let us consider each of these principles.

Desire

This the first step needed to gain a testimony. Enos provides a great example of how our desires can lead us to testimony. According to Enos, the words of his father concerning eternal life and the joy of the Saints sunk deep into his heart (Enos 1:3). Therefore, as Enos remembered the teachings of the gospel, these doctrines penetrated his soul. This is the key to testimony and conversion. It's not enough to know or understand the gospel intellectually. Like Enos, we must find ways to get the gospel into the hearts of our youth. That can only happen by the power of the Holy Ghost.

After the doctrines of the gospel settled into his heart, Enos declared, "And my soul hungered" (Enos 1:4). *Hunger* denotes a longing or craving for something. In the case of Enos, what he deeply desired was to know those things that his father knew. In order to gain testimonies of the gospel, our youth must want it like Enos did. If they don't desire a testimony, then, as parents, we must turn to the Lord to find ways of creating a need for our children to desire spiritual things.

Prayer

For Joseph Smith, the journey of testimony began by seeking God through the scriptures and inquiring of Him. Prayer is the key that unlocks the door and lets Christ into our lives. Sadly, many of the prayers of our youth—and perhaps even adults—are often trite and mechanical. When we pray, we should go to a secluded place where we can be alone and focus on Heavenly Father. As we communicate with God, we should try to visualize Him and think of whom we are speaking to. We should be able to open up, share feelings, and talk to our Heavenly Father just as we would communicate with our best friend here on the earth. We can share with Him our deepest secrets, desires, hopes, and dreams. Not only should we learn to talk with Him as we would a dear friend, but we must learn to listen to Him—that is where answers come.

If our youth can learn to pray in this manner, they will feel the Lord's presence and enjoy the companionship of the Spirit. As they learn of Him, He will direct their lives and help them walk the path of peace and safety. As they seek the Lord, He will reveal Himself to them through the Holy Ghost. Every truth of the gospel can be learned though the medium of prayer. The Lord has repeatedly invited us in the scriptures, "Ask, and it shall be given you; seek, and ye shall find; knock, and it shall be opened unto you" (Matthew 7:7). He wants us to ask; He wants us to seek, and if we do, He will reveal His will to us.

Study

If we want to gain a testimony of the gospel, we must read, study, and ponder the scriptures and the words of the living prophets. Our faith is strengthened as we immerse ourselves in the word of God (see Romans 10:17). From the Book of Mormon, we learn that "the preaching of the word had a great tendency to lead the people to do that which was just—yea, it had had more powerful effect upon the minds of the people than the sword, or anything else, which had happened unto them—therefore Alma thought it was expedient that they should try the virtue of the word of God" (Alma 31:5).

Alma understood the power of the scriptures. He also understood that if the people were taught the word, they would draw closer to the Savior and repent of their sins. We want our youth to immerse themselves in the scriptures because true doctrine changes lives. As our youth read and study the gospel, their testimonies will grow and their conversion will deepen. Furthermore, they will learn the doctrine, feel the Spirit, receive answers to their prayers, and begin to incorporate Christlike traits in their lives. Indeed, there is great strength to be gained by scripture study. Identifying with the ancient prophets and applying their teachings can help a child overcome their own personal problems. Therefore, if we want our youth to gain testimonies, they must read from the Book of Mormon daily. They must study the scriptures and put into practice the things they are reading.

Practice

It's one thing to know the gospel, but an entirely different thing to live Christ's teachings. Jesus taught, "My doctrine is not mine, but his that sent me. If any man will do his will, he shall know of the doctrine, whether it be of God, or whether I speak of myself" (John 7:16–17). The only way to really understand the gospel is true is to live it. A youth can't really know that Thomas S. Monson is a prophet until they study his messages and live the principles that he teaches. Likewise, an adult cannot comprehend the Atonement unless they have pled with the Lord for forgiveness and had to rely on the mercy of Christ for forgiveness.

None of us can know a doctrine is true until we live it. In the case of Enos, he didn't gain his testimony until he began to keep the commandments of God. By obedience to commandments, Enos was able to feel and respond to the promptings of the Holy Ghost.

THE PARENTS' ROLE IN HELPING CHILDREN GAIN A TESTIMONY

When children become teenagers, they must come to know if the gospel is true on their own. They can no longer take the word of their parents. President Harold B. Lee stated to youth, "The time is here when each of you must stand on your own feet. Be converted, because no one can endure on borrowed light. You will have to be guided by the light within yourself. If you do not have it, you will not stand."[7] Our youth need to become spiritually independent and stand on their own. The sooner they learn the gospel is true and seek for their own answers, they better prepared they are for becoming men and women of Christ.

However, often where parents fall short in helping their children gain testimonies is sharing their own with their children. We believe that one critical way that parents help their children gain solid testimonies is to create a home environment where testimonies can be shared—from parent to child, child to parent, and sibling to sibling—with ease, genuineness, and comfort. If you, as parents, have not shared your testimony recently with your children, now is the time!

Though there are many parents in the Church who actively teach their children the gospel, fewer seem comfortable testifying. Elder David A. Bednar asked, "Brethren and sisters, when was the last time you bore testimony to your eternal companion? Parents, when was the last time you declared your witness to your children about the things you know to be true? And children, when was the last time you shared your testimony with your parents and family?"[8] Children who are raised in Latter-day Saint homes should hear their parents testify of the truthfulness of the gospel. Wise parents will share their testimonies around the family fireside, but also during one-on-one occasions with their children. There should be both formal and informal settings in home life where testimony bearing takes place.

Several years ago, a father we know drove from his home in Mesa, Arizona, to Provo, Utah, to visit his three sons who were attending Brigham Young University. When asked why he made the 1,300-mile trip there and back in the middle of the week, the father responded, "I realized that it's been a while since I have shared my testimony with my sons. I wanted to come up and spend some time with them, and share my testimony." This father understood the power of testimony, and his sons will never forget the experience.

Testimonies borne in the home don't necessarily need to be eloquent or wordy. They could be as simple as saying, "Tithing is a true principle," or, "I am so grateful for Joseph Smith and what he did." Elder Vaughn J. Featherstone declared that as true disciples of Jesus Christ, "we ought to testify every day in every Latter-day Saint home to our [spouses], siblings, and children. These are the people we should love most on this earth. These are those we want to know the truth of this mighty work."[9]

Elder Featherstone then shared the following examples of how this could happen in the home.

> For example, a son may say to us, "I sure think President [Monson] is a good man."
> We could say, "Indeed, he is wonderful."
> What if instead we said, "Son, I know he is a prophet of God, a seer, and a revelator. He may be one of the greatest prophets that ever lived."
> Can you see the difference? Can you feel the difference? . . .
> Children need to hear their parents testify. Siblings can strengthen each other, and their friends can be lifted spiritually.
> Can you think of anything in this generation that would affect members of the Church more than living to be worthy of the Holy Ghost constantly and testifying as guided and directed by the Holy Ghost of the truth of this great, majestic, divine work and more especially of Him whose work this is?[10]

When parents testify to their children, spirit communicates with spirit and the gospel is transmitted from the heart of an adult to the heart of a child. When the gospel can sink deep into the hearts of our youth, their behaviors change and they desire to become more like Christ. Moreover, when the gospel is in their hearts, they are motivated to make wise choices because their desires are to do good. Values and beliefs can be transmitted from person to person, heart to heart, when the Holy Ghost is present. The Holy Ghost becomes the medium by which gospel knowledge flows.

GOSPEL GROWTH COMES FROM PARTICIPATION

One of the reasons missionaries become so deeply converted to the gospel is because of their daily involvement with the cause. In some remote geographic locations in the world, the missionaries really *are* the Church. Elder Neal A. Maxwell wisely observed, "Church members did not become inactive while crossing the plains, when the sense of belonging and being needed was so profound."[11] Likewise, our missionaries—and our youth—will not fall away or become inactive if they are participants in building the kingdom of God on earth.

One of the ways to prepare our youth to be strong missionaries is to keep them involved in the Church. In fact, when compared to other denominations, LDS youth are often more involved in their religion. From the *National Study of Youth and Religion,* researcher Kenda Creasy Dean found that more than half of all LDS youth (fifty-three percent) reported giving a presentation in church in the past six months (fewer than one in seven Southern Baptists and only one in twenty-five Catholic youth had done the same). Moreover, almost half (forty-eight percent) of Mormon teens had attended a meeting during the past six months where they were part of making decisions (as compared to one in four Southern Baptists and one in twelve Catholic teens). Also, our Latter-day Saint youth are more likely than other teens to participate in mission trips (seventy percent), share their faith with someone not of their faith (seventy-two percent), participate in religious youth groups (seventy-five percent), and speak publicly about their faith in a religious service or meeting (sixty-five percent). Kendra Dean called the LDS youth the "spiritual athletes" of their generation for their sacrifices, discipline, and energy. Her conclusion on LDS teens was positive, explaining:

> In nearly every area, using a variety of measures, Mormon teenagers were consistently the most positive, the most healthy, the most hopeful, and the most self-aware teenagers in the study. Mormon young people

also showed the highest degree of religious vitality and salience, the greatest degree of understanding of church teaching, and the highest degree of congruence between belief and action.[12]

As good as this is, there is still a need to have our youth even more involved than they are. Sure, we are doing great when compared to other religions; however, our standard for participation and outcomes that lead to conversion is perhaps higher than other faiths. If we want our children to become deeply converted to the gospel, they must be active participants and not mere spectators. After all, *this is their Church too, not just ours as adults.* Too often in the Church, youth leaders run programs, fill assignments, and conduct the meetings our youth should be conducting. Maybe such leaders simply feel it is easier to just do it rather than train youth to be leaders and become responsible.

Even in our homes, too often parents are doing all of the work while, once again, the children are observers. Our youth need to hear the gospel, yes, but they need to teach it as well. Our teens need great Church leaders, but they also need to do some of the leading. They are the future leaders of the Church and the future parents of the next generation. They can only be as good as our help to them! If we want them to become powerful teachers of the gospel in the mission field, they must begin teaching in the home.

Remember, conversion comes through participation. Who learns the most when they prepare a talk for sacrament meeting? Who learns the most when they prepare a lesson to give in church? We all understand that the instructors, teachers, or speakers are the one who benefit the most from the process. Therefore, we must place our youth in these roles where they can benefit the most from the service.

The gospel of Jesus Christ is true. Jesus Christ is at the helm. Joseph Smith ushered in a new dispensation. The Book of Mormon is the word of God. We have a living prophet who speaks to the Lord today and reveals His will to us. If our youth can come to know these things in their hearts, their lives will change forever. They will make a huge difference in this world and change it for the better.

PRACTICAL APPLICATION

- Give each family member a copy of the booklet *True to the Faith*. If you don't have access to the booklet, it can be downloaded

at https://www.lds.org/bc/content/shared/content/english/
pdf/language-materials/36863_eng.pdf. Study the section on
testimonies that begins on page 178.

- In a family home evening, teach about testimonies. There is a
wealth of resources provided on this topic from a keyword search
of "testimony." In your discussion, ask your children, "How does
a person act if they have a testimony of the gospel compared to
someone who doesn't have a testimony?"
- Have your children write their testimonies in copies of the Book
of Mormon to send to a nonmember or someone less active in
the Church.
- In a family council, discuss the topic of prayer and ask family
members how they could improve the quality of their own prayers.
- Parents, if you haven't shared your testimonies, find a way to
create a family culture where such sharing is normal and natural.

SUPPLEMENTAL MATERIALS

1. LDS Youth Site, "How Do I Gain a Testimony," https://www.
   lds.org/youth/video/how-do-i-gain-a-testimony?lang=eng.

2. Robert D. Hales, "Gaining a Testimony of God the Father; His
   Son, Jesus Christ; and the Holy Ghost," *Ensign*, May 2008.

3. Cecil B. Samuelson, "Testimony," *Ensign*, May 2011.

4. Mormon Messages, "Parenting: Touching the Hearts of Our
   Youth," Robert D. Hales; http://www.mormonchannel.org/video/
   mormon-messages?v=910947650001.

5. *True to the Faith*, "Testimony," 178–180; http://www.lds.org/
   manual/true-to-the-faith/testimony?lang=eng.

6. LDS Youth Site, "Trial of Your Faith," Neil L. Andersen; https://
   www.lds.org/youth/video/trial-of-your-faith?lang=eng.

REFERENCES

1. M. Russell Ballard, "Pure Testimony," *Ensign*, November 2004,
   40.

2. Spencer W. Kimball, "When the World Will Be Converted," *Ensign*, October 1974.

3. Ibid.

4. Christian Smith and Melinda Lundquist Denton, *Soul Searching: The Religious and Spiritual Lives of American Teenagers* (Oxford University Press: New York, 2005), 37.

5. Harold B. Lee, "Testimony," *Church News*, July 15, 1972, 4.

6. John A. Widtsoe, *Improvement Era*, May 1945, 273.

7. Harold B. Lee, "When Your Heart Tells You Things Your Mind Does Not Know," *Ensign*, April 1978.

8. David A. Bednar, "More Diligent and Concerned at Home," *Ensign*, November 2009, 19.

9. Vaughn J. Featherstone, "Things Too Wonderful for Me," Brigham Young University 2000–2001 Speeches (BYU Publications and Graphics: Provo, Utah, 2001), 171–72.

10. Ibid., 176–77.

11. Neal A. Maxwell, "A Brother Offended," *Ensign*, May 1982.

12. Kenda Creasy Dean, *Almost Christian: What the Faith of Our Teenagers Is Telling the American Church* (Oxford University Press: New York, 2010), 56–57, 203.

CHAPTER 6
GETTING CONVERTED

"The most important responsibility that we, as members of the Church of Jesus Christ, have is to see that we are converted to the truthfulness of the gospel."[1]

—Harold B. Lee

WHILE THE MOST important convert that most missionaries gain in the Lord's service is themselves, think of the potential benefits of the missionary who is strongly converted to the gospel before he or she leaves for the MTC. One of us had a conversation with a returned sister missionary who presently teaches at the MTC in Provo, Utah. She mentioned that ideally MTC instructors are supposed to be helping their missionaries acquire a language and learn to become powerful gospel teachers. Instead, she said, the instructors spend most of their time teaching the gospel to the new missionaries and helping them gain testimonies and become converted.

Just think of the opportunities that have been lost because of these sorts of situations. Instead of new missionaries learning from masterful and experienced former missionaries how to teach the gospel, they are simply learning the gospel itself. This is the equivalent of individuals who enroll in firefighter training school to learn from the best in the business the intricate details of putting out fires, but instead they spend all of their time learning what a fire is. As parents, we need to do a better job of helping our children become converted to the gospel while they are young.

More missionaries doesn't necessarily mean more convert baptisms, yet our hope as a Church is that the more missionaries we send out, the more people we can reach who will join the Church and enjoy the infinite blessings of the gospel. However, that hasn't happened. The following data shows the growth of the Church during the past thirty years. It also highlights the number of missionaries serving, as well as converts per missionary. As you can see, the proportion of missionaries to converts has actually decreased over time. It seems that more missionaries being sent out hasn't actually translated to more conversions per missionary.

Year	Missionaries	Convert Baptisms	Converts per Missionary
1984	27,655	192,983	6.9
1994	47,311	300,730	6.4
2012	58,990	272,330	4.6
2013	83,035	282,945	3.4

Before the historical announcement by President Monson, we had 58,990 missionaries. After the announcement, the missionary force grew to over 83,000. Therefore, our missionary force increased in one year by over 24,000 missionaries. That would have constituted the entire missionary force back in the late 70s and early 80s. This was a forty-two percent increase in the number of missionaries serving throughout the world, the most significant missionary force of our generation! However, in 2012 there were over 272,000 converts, and that number rose the following year to over 282,000. Though we increased in one year by over 10,000 new members, converts per missionary only increased by *four* percent. We don't claim to be statisticians and we certainly don't assert to have the answers to these issues; however, is it possible that one of the reasons that our increased missionary force isn't baptizing nearly as many people is because our missionaries are not as effective as they could be? Is it possible that if our missionaries were more prepared, more significantly converted, that the number of convert baptisms would be a little more commensurate with the number of missionaries serving? We present that as a possibility.

CONVERSION DRIVES BEHAVIOR

Several years ago, one of us visited with a man in his mid-twenties. At that point in his life, he had experienced many difficulties. He hadn't served a mission and had been involved in a number of deviant behaviors, including a host of sexual sins and drug habits. Presently, he was dealing with a pornography addiction, which he said was much more difficult to shake than his drug addictions. However, as a youth, this man had been an Eagle Scout and a seminary graduate. When asked what went wrong and how he'd drifted so far off course, his response was, "I guess I really just never was converted to the gospel."

Indeed, like with testimonies, *conversion also drives behavior*. Our conversion to the gospel molds and shapes the decisions we make and the course of life we pursue. What good are the teachings of the Church if they don't inspire us and lift us to become disciples of Jesus Christ? Our youth know the gospel intellectually perhaps more than any previous generation. However, knowledge alone does not convert someone to the gospel; hence, mere knowledge does not save. Youth today, despite their gospel knowledge, are still plagued with sins, problems, addictions, and other sinful behaviors perhaps more than ever before. Many of these youth can quote scriptures on charity while they club their little brother over the head with a whiffle bat. Some can recite with amazing accuracy the Old Testament stories of David and Bathsheba, or better yet Joseph and Potiphar's wife, and yet not be worthy to partake of the sacrament on a given Sunday because of moral transgression. Some may be able to quote modern prophets or *For Strength of Youth* on modesty or sexual purity while wearing a bikini or while being plagued with a pornography addiction. No, you cannot be engaged in deviant behavior and be converted to the gospel at the same time. It just doesn't work like that. Why? Once again, because true conversion drives our behavior.

WHAT IS CONVERSION?

To be converted implies change and renewal. It means to become spiritually-minded and conquer our unrighteous desires. Through the conversion process, we are changed through the Savior's Atonement and by the power of the Holy Ghost. President Harold B. Lee stated, "To become converted, according to the scriptures, means having a change of heart and the moral character of a person turned from the controlled power of sin into a righteous life. . . . It means to overcome the tendencies to criticize and to strive continually to improve inward weaknesses and not merely the outward appearances."[2] Conversion suggests improving and changing ourselves so that we can become like Jesus Christ. When we are converted, not only does our behavior change, but so does our nature. We become more like the Savior, and we radiate His love and compassion to those around us. The true convert wants to learn more about the Savior, acquire His attributes, and act the way the Savior would act. Thus, the converted individual is more kind, loving, and compassionate while also being less critical, judgmental, and negative.

Therefore, when we become converted, we take upon ourselves not *only* the Savior's name, but also His attributes. When we become converted, we are willing to do the things that He asks of us. We hunger and thirst after righteousness and seek to know the will of God and His modern-day prophets and apostles. To be converted is to live each day by the influence and direction of the Holy Ghost.

TESTIMONY VERSUS CONVERSION

Being converted, however, and having a testimony of the gospel are two different things. It is one thing to believe. The devils also believe and tremble (James 2:19). Or in other words, Satan also knows that the gospel is true. Satan can testify that Joseph Smith restored the Church, that the Book of Mormon is the word of God, and that the plan of salvation is God's plan for our happiness. Yes, Satan knows all of that. It's not enough for our youth to simply believe, or even know. They must become! The gospel must move from their heads into their hearts.

Recently, Elder David A. Bednar spoke in general conference regarding the difference between testimony and conversion. Here are a few key points he shared:

- "Conversion is an enlarging, a deepening, and a broadening of the undergirding base of testimony."

- "Conversion is an offering of self, of love, and of loyalty we give to God in gratitude for the gift of testimony."
- "Conversion unto the Lord requires both persistence and patience."
- "Testimony is the beginning of and a prerequisite to continuing conversion."
- "Testimony is a point of departure; it is not an ultimate destination."
- "Testimony is important and necessary but not sufficient to provide the spiritual strength and protection we need."
- "Knowing that the gospel is true is the essence of a testimony. Consistently being true to the gospel is the essence of conversion."[3]

A testimony gives us knowledge that we didn't before have; being converted turns our knowledge into action. In John 6, Jesus taught doctrine that required a full commitment to God. Many of Jesus's followers left him at that point. However, when Jesus asked the Twelve Apostles if they would leave too, Peter forcefully declared, "Lord, to whom shall we go? thou hast the words of eternal life. And we believe and are sure that thou art that Christ, the Son of the living God" (John 6:68–69).

On another occasion, Peter testified to Jesus, "Thou art the Christ, the Son of the living God" (Matthew 16:16). However, despite these statements, Jesus later told Peter, "When thou art converted, strengthen thy brethren" (Luke 22:32). Thus, Peter knew intellectually that Jesus was the Messiah, but that testimony hadn't sunk into his heart and caused him to change. Peter's testimony did not guide his behavior; consequently, he did not stand up for his convictions. He denied that he knew the Savior several times. But once Peter became converted, he was an unstoppable force for good. He boldly testified and told the Jews they had killed the Christ and invited them all to be baptized (Acts 2:36–38). He continued to make bold declarations, inviting all to repent, and never backed down. Ultimately, Peter was crucified and died as a martyr. He left this earth as a rock-solid citizen in the Lord's kingdom—converted to the core.

SHOT-IN-THE-ARM CONVERSION

Many parents can be fooled into thinking that if they can just get their son or daughter to youth conference, EFY, or a pioneer trek of some sort, then they will be converted to the gospel and live happily ever after. When some of these youth come home from such spiritual highs, families are elated. Sinners have become saints over the course of a weekend! However, many parents become disappointed when reality sets in, which is usually somewhere between two hours to two days after the youth have returned from their wonderful adventure. In some ways, these experiences are like ingesting some kind of energy drink. For several hours, a person can operate at peak performance, but once the spiritual energy burns off, individuals can turn back into what they were before quite quickly.

One father related to us that his son who had been in counseling for months was now completely cured. After a week at *one* of these previously mentioned activities, he had changed from his sexually deviant lifestyle and rebellious attitude into a stripling warrior. However, two weeks later, the father called and asked for another counseling appointment. His son was once again out of control and unmanageable.

Shot-in-the-arm dramatic conversions do not last. Please don't misunderstand. We believe there is great value in youth conferences, treks, EFY, and other such activities. Our children have all attended these events, and we have participated as speakers. What we are saying is that conversion is a process, not an event. There are many different experiences that will impact a child's conversion, not just one. Therefore, EFY and youth conferences are part of the conversion process, but left alone, they will fall short. These events are great supports for those youth who already have testimonies, but they can't stand alone in the conversion process.

As President Spencer W. Kimball would say, such events are like another drop of oil in the lamp. Over time, a lamp filled with oil will help someone make his or her way through the darkness. Solid and consistent gospel study, prayer, and service to others will do more for a youth over time than pulling a handcart through the desert. Now, couple the consistency of prayer and scripture study—for example—with a handcart trek and the environment has been created for spiritual experiences to occur.

What the youth really need is consistency. Instead of shot-in-the-arm conversions, they need steady and consistent gospel living. From *True to the Faith*, we learn, "Conversion is a process, not an event. You become converted as a result of your righteous efforts to follow the Savior. These efforts include exercising faith in Jesus Christ, repenting of sin, being baptized, receiving the gift of the Holy Ghost, and enduring to the end in faith."[4] Elder Bruce R. McConkie shed more light on this subject when he declared,

> A person may get converted in a moment, miraculously. That is what happened to Alma the Younger. He had been baptized in his youth, he had been promised the Holy Ghost, but he had never received it. He was too worldly-wise; he went off with the sons of Mosiah to destroy the Church. . . . In his instance the conversion was miraculous, in the snap of a finger, almost. . . . But that is not the way it happens with most people. With most people, conversion is a process; and it goes step by step, degree by degree, level by level, from a lower state to a higher, from grace to grace, until the time that the individual is wholly turned to the cause of righteousness. Now this means that an individual overcomes one sin today and another sin tomorrow. He perfects his life in one field now, and in another field later on. And the conversion process goes on, until it is completed, until we become, literally, as the Book of Mormon says, saints of God instead of natural men.[5]

For example, several years ago, Elder Gerald Lund shared the experience of a girl who felt that she did not have a testimony. She began to fast every other day. Not only did she deeply desire a witness, but she wanted a dramatic display and a "Pentecostal-like" spiritual outpouring. One day, in tears, she related to her father, "I don't have a testimony." Her father wondered how she came up with such an idea. She opened up her heart and revealed, "Because I have never experienced anything like Alma the Younger, or Paul, or King Lamoni." Elder Lund then made this plea to those who are teaching the gospel:

> It is unfortunate, it makes me weep, that inadvertently, we who are teaching the gospel sometimes make our youth feel that if their conversion is not dramatic, if it is not remarkable, then it is not true. When you teach the Book of Mormon, you teach Alma and Lamoni. But you remind them that for every Alma the Younger there were a thousand unnamed Saints who just lived good lives and who lived righteously from the time they were young. For every King Lamoni

there were thousands of Lamanites who didn't have to go into a trance or an unconscious state; they just heard his words and believed and were converted.[6]

Again, conversion isn't a one-time shot in the arm. It's a process that takes a lifetime. Teach your children to look for the quiet answers, the subtle evidence of God in their lives. Teach them to be consistent in living the gospel—that is the essence of conversion.

THE FAMILY'S ROLE IN CONVERSION

The home is the laboratory of love. It's a classroom where convictions are strengthened and the gospel is taught in pureness and simplicity. There is no better place to plant the seeds of testimony than in the home. The role of the Church isn't to supplant what is taught in the home, but to reinforce the spiritual teachings of parents. In order for the gospel to be taught, loved, accepted, and lived, the message must be delivered in a customized, personal way.

No one knows your children better than you do. Teach them on their levels, but also teach them according to their personalities. Connect with them! Because parents today are so busy, they often parent their children in the "herd" mentality. That is to say, every gospel discussion and teaching moment is in the presence of other family members. When was the last time you had a gospel discussion with one of your children, just you and that child? We would invite you to try this approach. You and your child will get more spiritual mileage out of this experience than twenty family home evenings. The best way that you can help your children become converted to the gospel is to have a strong relationship with them. If you are connected to your children emotionally, you can teach and influence them in powerful ways. They will come to you for answers to their questions, and you will share personal experiences with them that distill upon their minds and hearts. Conversely, if you *don't* have that kind of relationship with your children, your influence will be limited. There is little teaching that will occur in their hearts if your relationship with them is shoddy and impersonal. In fact, if this is the case, your children will have little desire to become converted because of you.

When we ran an informal survey to LDS institute students in Texas several years ago, the majority of them said that their conversion to the gospel could be attributed to the spiritual example and positive relationship with one or both of their parents. Parental example and connection cannot be emphasized enough in the conversion process. For example, a grandmother from Utah, reflecting back on her own childhood, wrote of her parents, "Just knowing I was loved and valued as a daughter primarily contributed to me buying into what my parents taught." Another mother from Texas, thinking back, shared with us, "What my parents thought of me mattered more than what my peers thought. Even though we didn't have family home evening every week, I felt like my parents were teaching me daily. I always knew they loved me." Once children feel from their parents that they are loved and accepted, they are then ready to have the gospel enter into their hearts.

Remember, no one can teach your children better than you can, especially if you are prayerful and seek the Lord's guidance. No teacher understands what your children are like when they have bad days, or when they feel rejected or down. Only you can understand exactly what your children are going through and experiencing. With that knowledge, you can teach them powerful, lasting lessons. You know what they need. Open your heart and share the gospel message with them in a personal way. Tell them what the world was like when you were their age. Share with them some of your struggles, questions, and doubts. Show them how you overcame your challenges. Teach them how the Lord blessed your life. They won't forget these meetings.

When we asked a thirty-six-year-old man from California who was most instrumental in helping him gain a testimony as a youth, he wrote,

> I remember seeing my mom praying and my dad would always get teary bearing his testimony. My mom was also consistent in trying to do the things that we should be doing—family prayer, family scripture study, and family home evening. We were never perfect, but she would be inspired after a good talk in Church or general conference and we would go at it for several weeks, or a month or two, and then slowly begin to drift off course. However, another Church talk or conference message would always get us back on track. Fast forward one generation, and with my own children we never miss family home evening, we never miss family prayer, and we never miss family scripture study.

When we asked a thirty-year-old woman from Texas what her parents did to help impact her testimony as a youth, she related,

> We always read scriptures together and prayed together every night. We always had family home evening even though it was hard to get together and most of us didn't want to. My parents were always strong in their Church callings. My parents were never shy to admit their feelings about the Church, how they knew it was true, or how it had changed their lives. They would always bear their testimony to us.

We also had the chance to interview the mother of this thirty-year-old Texas woman. We asked her what she and her husband did to help their children get the gospel deep in their hearts, to which she responded,

> Our family has been accused many times of spending too much time sitting in a circle and just talking and laughing. We have even skipped activities or other Church events because our discussions have gone on for hours. I truly feel this has been a great bonding experience for our family and we have become united in building our testimonies through sharing our feelings about the gospel with each other. Our family home evenings can easily turn from twenty-minute lessons to three-hour discussions.

Truly, the family (especially parents) can play a key role in helping our youth get the gospel deep into their hearts. From the previous comments, it's easy to see that having a strong relationship is the most important foundational piece in order for teaching to take place. With a strong, positive relationship, parents can assist their children in the conversion process.

What signs or indicators can parents look for to determine if their children are becoming converted to the gospel? An obvious answer would be their demeanor: the lights in their eyes and their positive outlooks on life. Expressing their testimonies publicly and privately, reading their scriptures, praying, attending their meetings, and having a desire to be good and live the gospel would all be indicators that the work of conversion in underway. If your children are generally mean and ornery, look for them making an effort to be kind and Christlike. If they are proud and self-centered, you may notice that they're beginning to be aware others around them and are becoming humble and selfless. In *True to the Faith*, there are other indicators of conversion listed, originating from the Book of Mormon.

- They desire to do good (Mosiah 5:2)
- They do not rebel against the Lord (Alma 23:6)
- They are filled with love (4 Nephi 1:2, 15–17)[7]

ROUGH AND TOUGH

The world is becoming increasingly sinful, wicked, and perverse. Conditions will likely only get worse. However, we are confident that the Lord will help raise up a generation of young people that will be equal to the challenge. Several years ago, President Henry B. Eyring spoke to religious educators regarding conversion. He also spoke, in a tone of soberness, about the conditions of the world. He declared,

> Our concern is deepened by what we know it will take to be a missionary and a parent in the days ahead. It will take deep conversion to the gospel of Jesus Christ. It will take the companionship of the Holy Ghost. And wickedness is the tool of the enemy against that conversion and that companionship. True conversion, where the gospel of Jesus Christ goes deep into the heart and changes it, brings the companionship of the Holy Ghost. One of the dangers of the times we are passing into is that we might be tempted to lower our expectations for ourselves and for those young people we serve. As the world darkens, even a partial conversion and a few spiritual experiences may seem more and more remarkable, compared to the world. We might be tempted to expect less.[8]

Yes, the world will become dark, but we must not let that drag our youth down. Elder Richard G. Scott said, "True conversion yields the fruit of enduring happiness that can be enjoyed even when the world is in turmoil and most are anything but happy."[9] No matter how sick and problematic the world becomes, those youth who have paid the price to become deeply converted will be able to smile despite the less-than-favorable conditions. Those who are converted will be at peace and will be happy because they will always have the Spirit with them.

In such a wicked world, our youth need to become strong in the gospel. They need to be able to stand on their own two feet spiritually. They cannot rely on the testimonies of their parents, friends, or Church leaders. President Harold B. Lee stated, "The time is here when each of you must stand on your own feet. Be converted, because no one can endure on borrowed light. You will have to be guided by the light within yourself. If you do not have it, you will not stand."[10] Only those with rock-solid testimonies will remain pure and true. In the end, all that will matter is what we are made of and what we've done with it.

Indeed, as parents we cannot hold our children's hands and walk them safely to the path of righteousness when they are adults. We have to teach them correct principles and pray that they will learn to govern themselves!

If our youth can enter the mission field, on fire, converted and ready to roll, they will make such a difference in the lives of everyone who will listen to them.

PRACTICAL APPLICATION

- As a family, study "conversion" in the Topical Guide and the Church magazines. Decide what steps must be taken to become stronger Church members, more deeply converted to the gospel.
- Select a Church history site to visit or take a vacation too. If your children have never been to Palmyra, Kirtland, Independence, Nauvoo, or on the trails of Wyoming, you may want to consider something along those lines. Find ways to emphasize your deep feelings about the gospel on these occasions.
- If you have teenage children, see if several members of your family can go on exchanges with the missionaries. Begin now to learn what missionary work is all about.
- Discuss in a family council ways to have a gospel-centered home, and then implement those changes.
- If you haven't done so yet, help your children find names of their ancestors that they can be baptized for in the temple. Discuss how family history work can help all of us become more converted to the gospel.

SUPPLEMENTAL RESOURCES

1. David A. Bednar, "Converted unto the Lord," *Ensign*, November 2012.

2. Bonnie L. Oscarson, "Be Ye Converted," *Ensign*, November 2013.

3. Richard G. Scott, "Full Conversion Brings Happiness," *Ensign*, May 2002.

4. *True to the Faith*, "Conversion," http://www.lds.org/manual/true-to-the-faith/conversion?lang=eng.

5. Video: "Waiting on Our Road to Damascus," Dieter F. Uchtdorf, http://www.lds.org/media-library/video/2012-01-003-waiting-on-our-road-to-damascus?lang=eng.

REFERENCES

1. Harold B. Lee, *Stand Ye in Holy Places* (Deseret Book: Salt Lake City, 1974), 90.

2. Ibid., 354–55.

3. David A. Bednar, "Converted unto the Lord," *Ensign*, November 2012, 107–9.

4. *True to the Faith: A Gospel Reference* (2004), 41.

5. Bruce R. McConkie, "Be Ye Converted," from an address at BYU First Stake Conference, February 11, 1968; see also excerpts from an address at BYU in 1976, as cited in J. F. McConkie & R. L. Millet, *Doctrinal Commentary on the Book of Mormon*, Vol. 2 (Salt Lake City: Bookcraft, 1988), 174–75.

6. Gerald N. Lund, *Selected Writings of Gerald N. Lund: Gospel Scholars Series* (Salt Lake City: Deseret Book, 1999), 384.

7. *True to the Faith: A Gospel Reference* (2004), 42–43.

8. Henry B. Eyring, "Raising Expectations," CES Satellite Training Broadcast, August 2004.

9. Richard G. Scott, "Full Conversion Brings Happiness," *Ensign*, May 2002, 24.

10. Harold B. Lee, *Stand Ye in Holy Places* (Deseret Book: Salt Lake City, 1974), 95.

CHAPTER 7
RECEIVING ANSWERS
FROM THE SPIRIT

"Let all persons be fervent in prayer, until they know the things of God for themselves and become certain that they are walking in the path that leads to everlasting life."[1]

—Brigham Young

MISSIONARIES LEARN THE importance, value, and sacredness of personal prayer. While on a mission, an elder or sister will pray more than they have at any other time of their lives. Missionaries pray when they wake up, before they eat, before they leave their apartments, before they begin knocking on doors, before they speak in Church, before they teach a lesson, before they plan their day, and before they retired to bed. In fact, missionaries "pray without ceasing" (1 Thessalonians 5:17). One of the greatest lessons in the life of a missionary is that he or she cannot do the Lord's work without His help.

Missionaries must do more than pray. They must learn to receive answers to prayer from the Holy Ghost. It is that Spirit that guides and directs a missionary in his or her daily ministry. Through the Holy Ghost, a missionary receives answers to his or her prayers, is directed to where he or she should proselyte, is able to teach with power and authority, and is then able to indentify the Spirit to the investigators whom he or she teaches. Understanding the Spirit and following it is absolutely paramount to the happiness, success, and fulfillment of every missionary.

One of the most important things parents can do for their children is teach them how to pray sincerely and how to receive answers to their prayers. Parents would also do well to help their children understand the different ways the Holy Ghost can manifest Himself.

Regarding answers to prayers, consider Alma the Younger. When he went on a mission to visit the Zoramites, he was astonished to find apostate Nephites worshiping idols. Even worse, their brand of worship excluded the poor, who were left believing that, without access to the synagogues, they couldn't pray. "What shall these my brethren do," asked a spokesman, "for they are despised of all men because of their poverty . . . and we have no place to worship our God" (Alma 32:5)?

Alma's response is a classic sermon of how anyone, regardless of circumstance or age, can gain a witness of truth. It also becomes a primer for how parents can help their children gain the type of testimony that holds up to the fiercest of storms. Alma first helped these humble people know what to expect: "Now, as I said concerning faith—that it was not a perfect knowledge—even so it is with my words. Ye cannot know of their surety at first, unto perfection, any more than faith is a perfect knowledge" (Alma 32:26).

Thus, Alma explained that gaining faith—like learning to receive answers to prayer—is a process. It will take time, learning what to feel and what to expect. Spiritual muscles grow as they are used and developed. Alma further explained, "If ye will awake and arouse your faculties, even to an experiment upon my words, and exercise a particle of faith, yea, even if ye can no more than desire to believe," then "this desire [will] work in you" (Alma 32:27).

PRAYER TAKES EFFORT

Million-dollar answers don't come from ten-cent prayers. Brigham Young taught, "Prayer is often difficult and strenuous—just plain hard work. If you really want to converse with the Lord, you must count on a mighty struggle. Receiving inspiration and revelation through prayer is one of the greatest achievements of man, and to expect that blessing without effort is contrary to the order of heaven."[2] Indeed, prayer takes work and effort. As adults, we pray most fervently when we have something to pray about, when we are struggling with a great need, for ourselves or for others.

Children are the same way. The best time for them to learn how to pray and receive answers is when there is a specific answer they are looking for. They are most teachable when they have a desire to solve a real problem. Brigham Young further taught, "One has to break the prayer barrier by knocking and knocking. We should not be dismayed when much knocking at first seems to avail little. There are few exercises in faith greater than that of praying persistently."[3] Parents, teach your children to be persistent in prayer, as that is when the greatest answers seem to come.

Regardless of age, children have a constant laundry list of needs and desires. Grades, friends, dating, futures, missions, bullies, standards, and sports all present problems that need solving. And, as we've talked about previously, their growth and maturity depends on learning to solve them. A wise child psychologist said that in any given year, millions of drills were sold to people who didn't want drills. They just wanted holes. Put another way, too many of our members expect million-dollar answers to ten-cent prayers.

PRAYER AND CONVERSION

Preparing a child to pray and receive answers, then having the courage to follow those answers, is the essence of converting children to the gospel. Everything else is secondary. In order for this to occur, parents and teachers need to stay focused on helping children experience the following events:

- Knowing and feeling that God really loves them.
- Coming to understand God's "characteristics and attributes" (see *Lectures on Faith*). This means, among other things, it is His great desire to become the "speaker of all our words and the door of all our deeds."
- Being able to identify the Holy Ghost when it speaks to them.
- Recognizing the Spirit as a manifestation of His love and awareness of them.

- Having experiences following the directions of the Spirit and seeing the result.

If children don't have their own personal spiritual experiences, then they will have sat in hundreds of hours of Primary, Sunday School, Young Men or Young Women, firesides, family home evenings, and a host of other meetings, and yet never have completely connected with Heavenly Father. Unfortunately, because there is a price to be paid when it comes to hearing the Lord's voice, many adults in the Church—parents of our youth—have shallow roots when it comes to the gospel.

In *Preach My Gospel*, we learn to better understand the role of prayer and how the Lord speaks to us:

> In prayer we speak openly and honestly with our loving Father in Heaven. We express gratitude and thanksgiving for our blessings. We may acknowledge our love for Him. We also ask for help, protection, and direction according to our needs.
>
> As we pray with faith, sincerity, and real intent, we will see God's influence in our lives. He will guide us in our daily lives and help us make good decisions. He will bless us with feelings of comfort and peace. He will warn us of danger and strengthen us to resist temptation. He will forgive our sins. We will feel closer to Him. We must learn to recognize His influence in our lives. We must learn to listen to the still, small voice of the Spirit.
>
> We can recognize when the Holy Ghost is teaching us the truth. Our minds will be filled with inspiring and uplifting thoughts. We will be enlightened, or given new knowledge. Our hearts will have feelings of peace, joy, and love. We will want to do good and be helpful to others. These feelings are hard to describe but can be recognized as we experience them.[4]

TEACHING CHILDREN TO PRAY

After returning from the mission to the Zoramites, Alma turned his attention to teaching the gospel to his sons. To Helaman, who would become high priest over the church, he advised, "O, remember, my son, and learn wisdom in thy youth" (Alma 37:35). Two verses later, he then told Helaman how to gain that wisdom: "Counsel with the Lord in all thy doings, and he will direct thee for good."

Both children and adults need to learn to counsel with the Lord in their doings. As former bishops and family counselors, we have met often with individuals who have come to receive counsel and direction. We would talk over issues and explore new options. These individuals often poured out their fears and worries. They often talk through past experiences that have worn them down physically, emotionally, and spiritually. In the end, we could give advice and counsel, but the responsibility still rested on the person to implement what we'd discussed.

Consider trying to communicate the immense importance of prayer to a thirteen-year-old girl. She would have much need of guidance and counsel. A teenager's frustrations about peer pressure, bodily changes, parents, and freedoms are constant and ever-changing. She would need counsel she could trust and a listening ear where she wouldn't feel she is being judged.

We can teach her how to pray in the way we suggest that she pray. How we say it is important.

Michelle: "Mom, my friends are being mean."

Mom: "What's happening?"

Michelle: "At school, they all huddle up and whisper. When I come walking up, they stop."

Mom: "What have you thought about doing?"

Michelle: "I don't know. They're just being mean!"

Mom: "Wow. That's hard. Have you talked with the Lord about it?"

Michelle: "No."

Mom: "Michelle, counsel with Him. Tell Him everything. If it'll help, I'll do the same thing. Let's see what kind of answers we get."

Michelle: "Okay. Thanks."

The more we speak of prayer in terms of counsel and guidance, the more we invite children to open up to the Lord beyond a rote list of memorized phrases. At that moment, the Lord becomes an active participant in their lives. Think of the blessings that will come into the lives of our future missionaries if they can learn early to "counsel with the Lord."

TEACHING CHILDREN WHAT TO LISTEN FOR

If we aren't careful, we can become locked into a single method for getting answers to prayers. One way of praying may have worked for someone else, so we might assume it should work for everyone, even though we all have different spiritual gifts. A good example of this is what we call the "Confirmation Method." When Oliver Cowdrey was given the opportunity to translate the Book of Mormon, the Lord indicated to him that he would know what was right by a "burning in the bosom." If he was *not* to take a certain course or path, he would experience a "stupor of thought" (D&C 9:8–9). For many in the Church, the confirmation—burning or stupor—works well. But it does not work that way for everyone.

For example, shortly after leaving Egypt, the children of Israel were terrified. In front of them was the Red Sea and coming from behind were the armies of Pharaoh. They needed to know what direction to go to be saved. They needed deliverance quickly! How were they to know what to do? In this case, the most logical of the possibilities was to either go north, toward more fertile lands, or south, deeper into the desert. Given their choices, it is reasonable to assume they would have chosen to go north. And yet, there was another possibility outside their experience, one that only a God would know—the parting of the Red Sea. Because of this plan, a loving Heavenly Father wouldn't have answered either of the possibilities with stupor or burning. He had a more complete plan they couldn't even conceive of.

The LDS Bible Dictionary states: "Prayer is the act by which the will of the Father and the will of the child are brought into correspondence with each other. The object of prayer is not to change the will of God but to secure for ourselves and for others blessings that God is already willing to grant but that are made conditional on our asking for them."[5]

In the case of the children of Israel standing at the Red Sea, they needed to be more focused on the will of the Father rather than trying to limit Him to the narrow possibilities within mortal understanding. Similarly, if our children understand the great love God has for them, they will be more anxious to discover His will, His solutions for them.

OUR OWN EXPERIENCES

One roadblock in helping children learn to pray and follow the Spirit involves our own experiences, attitudes, and beliefs as adults.

It's hard to teach what we don't believe ourselves. Our professional and Church experiences tell us that there are many active Latter-day Saints who doubt whether the Lord answers their prayers. Most of these good people believe He answers other people's prayers, just not theirs.

Meanwhile, others have felt their prayers were answered, followed the inspired counsel and direction, and ran into complete disaster. Because of those experiences, they question the answers they receive from the Spirit. These individuals ask for answers, pray for them, and then fear to follow the given guidance. Children notice when we struggle with our own prayer dilemmas. Teens especially are quick to spot hypocrisy—gaps between what adults are telling them and how adults live their own lives.

If we would teach a child to get answers to prayers, we need to first ask ourselves some pointed questions:

- What do I believe about prayer?
- Do I really believe my children will get answers to their prayers?
- As a parent or youth leader, what example do children see in my approach to personal problems and personal prayer?
- How are my own prayers? Do I "counsel with the Lord" or do I simply present a laundry list of problems before Him?
- Am I quick to spot the Lord's tender mercies and thank Him for them?

The link between a human child and Heavenly Father is personal prayer. Those who have personal spiritual experiences develop sustaining root systems that carry them through life's trials. Those that don't are constantly in danger of beginning challenged in a way they are unprepared for. In the entire conversion process, there is possibly no greater key than powerful prayers in the lives of our youth.

DIFFERENT WAYS TO FEEL HIS SPIRIT

Several years ago, one of our children (we'll keep her anonymous) came to us quite discouraged. After a Sunday at Church where every girl in Young Women was crying as they shared their testimony and every leader was as well, this child came home, saying, "I guess I don't have a testimony." Knowing that she was rock-solid in the gospel, the question was asked, "Why would you say that?" Her response, "Because everyone always cries in Church when they testify. I never do, so I must not have a testimony."

A discussion at the dinner table then ensued, and this particular daughter was taught three important truths: first, just because you cry doesn't mean you have a testimony or are even feeling the Spirit. When some people feel the Spirit, they shed tears. However, oftentimes when people cry, they may not be feeling the Spirit at all. Sometimes we call these "emotion-onies" rather than testimonies. They seem to be common in youth conferences and Girls' Camps across the country. Second, there are many different ways of feeling the Spirit, and you must learn how Heavenly Father speaks to you personally. Third, learning how the Spirit works in your life could take some time—perhaps a lifetime!

Elder Bruce R. McConkie taught,

> Revelation comes from God to man in various appointed ways, according to the laws ordained by the Almighty. The Lord appears personally to certain spiritually receptive persons; He speaks audibly by His own voice, on occasions, to those whose ears are attuned to the divine wavelength; angels are sent from His presence to minister to deserving individuals; dreams and visions come from Him to the faithful; He often speaks by the still small voice, the voice of the Spirit, the voice of prophecy and revelation . . . and He gives his mind and will to the receptive mortals in whatever ways seem appropriate as circumstances require.[6]

In fact, Sister Julie B. Beck said, "The ability to qualify for, receive, and act on personal revelation is the single most important skill that can be acquired in this life."[7] Learning to hear, feel, or recognize the promptings of the Holy Ghost is one of the greatest pursuits of our lives. It may take a while for our children—and their parents—to learn how the Holy Ghost communicates with them.

For example, in Doctrine and Covenants 8:1, we learn about the "asking formula." Individuals are to "ask in faith," have an "honest heart," and "believe that answers will come." In Doctrine and Covenants 9:7–8, we also learn that part of the formula is that we must study it out in our minds. The "answer formula" is just as simple. According to Doctrine and Covenants 8:2, we learn that the Lord will answer us with impressions or ideas that come to our minds and by feelings that come to our hearts.

Parents can teach their children that most revelation will come to them as *thoughts* and *ideas* to their minds. No crying, no emotion. Just simple thoughts and ideas. President David O. McKay taught, "To all faithful members of the Church who are in the line of their duty the Holy Ghost normally speaks through their conscience."[8] If our youth are in the line of their duty, doing what they should be doing, most revelation that comes to them will be in the form of ideas. Joseph Smith called this "pure intelligence" and said that the Spirit may give us "sudden strokes of ideas."[9]

Parents can also teach their children that the Holy Ghost may speak to them with warm, peaceful, comfortable feelings that they will feel in their hearts. Elder H. Burke Peterson taught, "Most answers from the Lord are felt in our heart as a warm comfortable expression, or they may come as thoughts to our mind. They come to those who are prepared and who are patient."[10]

President Spencer W. Kimball warned the members of the Church not to be so dramatic when it comes to feeling the Spirit. Often, we're looking for angels blowing trumpets to answer our prayers. President Kimball said that the Cumorah's and the Kirtland's were realities, but they were the exceptions to the rule. Most of today's revelation comes in the form of impressions or ideas, without spectacle or drama. Then President Kimball stated, "Always expecting the spectacular, many will miss entirely the constant flow of revealed communication."[11]

The following chart shows some of the different ways the Holy Ghost could speak to us, as well as where to find references to study as a family. As parents, we recommend that you study these references with your children and teach them how the Holy Ghost can work in their lives. Share with them personal experiences.

How the Holy Ghost Can Work within Us	Reference
The Spirit can speak peace to the mind	Galatians 5:22; D&C 6:23
The Spirit can give us understanding	Job 32:8
The Spirit can cause our bosoms to burn	Luke 24:32; D&C 9:6–9

The Spirit can tell us in our minds and hearts	D&C 8:2–3
The Spirit can come as a voice to our minds	1 Samuel 3:4–10
The Spirit can come as the Lord's voice	Enos 1:10; 3 Nephi 11:1–7
The Spirit can come as a still, small voice	1 Kings 19:12; D&C 85:6
The Spirit can lead us to do good	1 Nephi 4:6; D&C 11:12
The Spirit can occupy our minds and press upon our feelings	D&C 128:1
The Spirit can warn us or constrain us	1 Nephi 2:1–2; Alma 14:11; Acts 27:10–11
The Spirit can come in the form of a dream	Genesis 37, 40, 41; Matthew 2:12
The Spirit can enlighten our minds and fill us with joy	D&C 11:11; 76:10; Alma 24:30; 32:34; Psalm 19:8

As our wonderful youth live on the earth in these last days, it'll be imperative for them to seek the Spirit in their lives, to live worthy of the Spirit, and to follow the promptings wherever they may lead. Our belief is that the Spirit will lead us to places of safety and refuge. Moreover, as we recognize the Spirit in our lives, the seeds of conversion will take root. Many of our youth have felt the Spirit in their lives. They simply need a guide—a parent, teacher, or leader—to identify it and help them follow it. Teaching our youth to how to recognize the Spirit in their lives and receive answers to their prayers will prepare them to be successful missionaries and devoted disciples of Jesus Christ.

PRACTICAL APPLICATION

- As a family, study chapter 4 of *Preach My Gospel*. Look for the roles of the Holy Ghost, how it can be manifested, and how prayers are answered.
- In a family home evening, have members of your family share personal experiences of how prayers have been answered in their lives. Parents could share how major decisions have been made through prayer and fasting.

- Study the topic of "prayer" in *True to the Faith*.
- Before family prayers, ask your children whom your family should be praying for. This will help prayers be more meaningful to all involved.

SUPPLEMENTAL RESOURCES

1. David A. Bednar, "Receive the Holy Ghost," *Ensign*, November 2010.

2. David A. Bednar, "That We May Always Have His Spirit to Be with Us," *Ensign*, May 2006.

3. D. Todd Christofferson, "Strong Impressions of the Spirit," *New Era*, June 2013.

4. Jay E. Jensen, "Have I Received an Answer from the Spirit?" *Ensign*, April 1989.

5. Richard G. Scott, "Learning to Recognize Answers to Prayer," *Ensign*, November 1989.

6. LDS Youth Video, "Prophets and Revelation—Hearing His Voice," https://www.lds.org/youth/video/hearing-his-voice?lang=eng.

7. LDS Youth Video, "Need Answers? Go to the Source," https://www.lds.org/youth/video/origin?lang=eng.

REFERENCES

1. Brigham Young, *Journal of Discourses*. 26 vols. London: Latter-day Saints' Book Depot, 1854–86, 9:150.

2. Ibid., 13:155.

3. Ibid.

4. *Preach My Gospel: A Guide to Missionary Service* (2004), 73.

5. Bible Dictionary, "Prayer."

6. Bruce R. McConkie, *Mormon Doctrine* (Salt Lake City: Bookcraft, 1958), 643–44.

7. Julie B. Beck, "And upon the Handmaids in Those Days Will I Pour Out My Spirit," *Ensign*, May 2010, 11.

8. As cited in Stephen R. Covey, *The Divine Center* (Salt Lake City: Deseret Book, 2004), 180.

9. Joseph Smith, *Teachings of the Prophet Joseph Smith* (Salt Lake City: Deseret Book, 1976), 151.

10. H. Burke Peterson, in Conference Report, October 1973, 13.

11. Spencer W. Kimball, in Conference Report, Munich Germany Area Conference, 1973, 77.

CHAPTER 8
THE BLESSINGS OF WORK

"It is the eternal, inescapable law that growth comes only from work and preparation, whether the growth be material, mental, or spiritual. Work has no substitute."[1]

—J. Reuben Clark Jr.

PRESIDENT EZRA TAFT Benson once said, "One of the greatest secrets of missionary work is work! If a missionary works, he will get the Spirit; if he gets the Spirit, he will teach by the Spirit; and if he teaches by the Spirit, he will touch the hearts of the people and he will be happy. There will be no homesickness, no worrying about families, for all time and talents and interests are centered on the work of the ministry. Work, work, work—there is no satisfactory substitute, especially in missionary work."[2] According to President Benson, if missionaries work, they will have the Holy Ghost with them, they will teach by the Spirit, they will touch many lives, they will be happy, they will not be homesick, they will not worry about their families, and they will be focusing on the work before them! These are wonderful promises that can be claimed by all who will follow the prophet's counsel.

Missionary work isn't often easy. We are afraid that many young men or women who desire to serve falsely assume that they are going to

EFY or youth conference for a year and a half or two. No, missionaries wake up early and stay up late. They often work twelve- to fifteen-hour days. They walk long distances, ride their bikes across cities and towns, and climb long flights of stairs. Yes, missionaries are always moving. But not all of the work that they do is physical. There is a large quantity of mental concentration that goes into preparing to teach investigators customized lessons, working with members and priesthood leaders, and helping to train fellow missionaries. There is never a dull moment in the mission field, and to meet the demands of a mission, missionaries must have a strong work ethic.

Are your children up to these rigorous demands? Without question, many of our youth are physically ready for the task. However, there are also many who are not. Some experts argue that we live in a world where children are no longer assets but rather are liabilities. Instead of helping on the family farm or with the family business, most children today are consumers, not producers. In this role, tired and worn-out parents work exorbitant hours each week, trying to keep up with the demands of their children. Many from the *chosen generation* expect cars, laptops, iPhones, tablets, and wardrobes that cost more than a modest vacation for a large family! It also seems that children today expect their parents to provide fun and pleasure; hence, they would rather their parents become entertainment directors on cruise ships rather than mothers and fathers who teach values and principles.

With all the perks and thrills, one would think that this pampered generation would be just about the happiest group in the entire history of mankind. After all, many of today's kids aren't expected to do a whole ton of difficult things. For some LDS youth, their lives consist of texting hour after hour, making "intelligent" Facebook updates like "I'm bored," or posting pictures of themselves sleeping on Instagram. Yet when compared to previous generations, these youth seem more down and unhappy than ever before, becoming depressed, lazy, and unproductive. And more of these youth are on medication for mental issues than any other generation in our nation's history. Supposedly, these medications are meant to remedy depression, anxiety, and stiflingly short attention spans. Though in reality, doctors and parents are often found to be medicating poor performance or high-maintenance behaviors. It appears that freedom and wealth haven't exactly molded our children into the stripling warriors we'd hoped they would be.

YOUTH AND WORK

If we want to have our youth become rock-solid in the gospel, they need to learn how to work, persevere, and overcome challenges. Living the gospel is not always a cushy, easy thing. Oftentimes, keeping our covenants takes great effort and sacrifice. And there's the rub! Too often modern parents don't expect or require much from their children. If a child gets an A on an exam or makes his or her bed, sometimes there's practically an awards ceremony. At minimum, there will almost certainly be a "proud parent" Facebook post.

It will be difficult for children to develop strength, fortitude, and resilience if their parents are constantly walking in front of them, knocking down or aside every obstacle so that they will have a safe, healthy, and happy upbringing. Are these parents really doing their children any favors? How will children ever learn to function as strong, independent adults and productive citizens if their parents are walking behind them with a safety net or in front of them with a shield and sword? Dr. David Fassler, an adolescent psychiatrist, argues that today's teenagers haven't "had enough bad things happen to them . . . [and] that in order to learn how to cope with normal frustrations, with ups and downs, [children] have to first experience them."[3]

Recently, a Young Men's leader shared with us this experience:

Last summer, I had the opportunity, with another adult leader, to take a group of young men on a High Adventure. Though it was a great experience, I was somewhat disheartened because most of these young men—between fourteen and fifteen—did not know how to work at all. They had absolutely no clue! Out of the ten young men on that trip, only one helped without being asked or told what to do. Two young men would help if we asked them, or spelled out in black and white what needed to be done. The remaining young men were completely helpless when it came to working or helping. The other adult leader I was with joined me in deciding after several days that we would no longer pick up after the young men. So the last day when we left our campsite, we literally left behind hundreds of dollars of equipment and clothing because we refused to clean up after these pampered young men. It was evident to me that these young men had been raised in homes where their parents did all of the work and probably spent a lot of their time picking up after these young men. Unfortunately, it appeared that most of these boys had little responsibility at home, and their experience on the High Adventure was just a microcosm of their entire lives.

In a similar vein, a Young Women's leader shared this experience with us:

A few years ago, we—along with some of our children—went on a stake youth trek, complete with handcarts, sweltering heat, and authentic pioneer clothing. We walked over twenty miles in the scorching Oklahoma summer heat. Though the experience was great, I was amazed at how many of our youth were not in physical shape (more youth had to be put in the infirmary and receive medical attention than adults), how many were not capable of working, and how many flat out refused to help. It made me grateful that my own children had been taught those principles, and since they were in our group, they were a great help. Some of our youth were completely incapable of helping pull a handcart, set up a tent, or make dinner—and these were seventeen- and eighteen-year-old young men and women. The first night we arrived in camp after walking all day in blistering heat, we (meaning my husband, my three children, and I) began making dinner for our group of twelve or fifteen. We couldn't get one other person in our group to help. We even asked one girl—eighteen years old and bound for BYU—if she would help us. She said, "I don't work with knives. I may hurt myself." Such was the attitude of all of the youth in our group. While our family worked frantically finding firewood to build a fire and cutting up food for the dinner, the rest of these youth simply chitchatted and complained about their sore toes. Ironically, when it was time to eat, they all crashed through the line, leaving only a few scraps for us—the ones who made the dinner.

Some experts have called the current cohort of children "the pampered generation." Many of these children have been raised on a steady diet of video games, smartphones, Disney cruises, costly wardrobes, and fancy restaurants. In some cases, parents have raised children who are completely impotent and useless to society and the Church. Speaking of this tendency, one radio talk show host made the following observation:

The modern bubble-wrap mentality assumes that children are so frail and easily bruised that they have to be insulated from . . . life. No losing, no disappointments, no harsh reality checks. But a child who grows up in a bubble without developing any immunities to the outside world, a child raised in bubble wrap is not prepared for the symptoms of life: failure, frustration, and having to make choices tougher than the color of their new iPod sleeve.[4]

If the future missionary force is made up of lazy, selfish young men and women, mission presidents will be pulling their own hair out, fretting over how they will get the Lord's work done with such a weak group. If we want to turn our homes into missionary training centers, we need to begin by teaching our children how to work—and work hard.

TEACHING WORK AND RESPONSIBILITY

Elder Gene R. Cook wrote, "If children are raised with a poor attitude about work and do not learn to sustain themselves, they will be weak and dependent as adults. They may ultimately become a liability to society instead of making a real contribution."[5] We seriously doubt that such lazy people will ever become deeply converted to the gospel or serve successful missions. It's a basic truth that the best missionaries are the ones with the strongest work ethic.

Elder Joe J. Christensen described some of the current youth when he said,

Teaching children to work, to take responsibility, requires some creativity. Especially in urban settings, too many children are growing up in an environment where they do not have enough to do. They are like the thirteen-year-old boy who was asked what he did all day in the summer.

He said, "Well, I get up in the morning about ten or eleven. Then my mom gets me something to eat. Then maybe I'll go with some of the guys and play a little basketball, maybe watch TV, and then go down to the mall and "hang out" for a while—sorta watch the girls and stuff.

When asked what time he got to bed, he said, "Oh, usually about one or two o'clock. I go over to a friend's house and watch some videos. It's really neat, because my friend's mom told the guy at the video shop that it was all right for her son to check out any video he wanted—including R-rated."

We could feel great concern for the future of that young Latter-day Saint boy and his friends.[6]

Unfortunately, this scenario described by Elder Christensen is all too common today. We are surprised at how many young people go into the mission field or head off to college having never worked a day of their lives.

The late Elder Stephen B. Oveson of the Seventy said the following:

> As a mission president, I saw a lot of young men come into the mission field who had never paid tithing. They taught investigators the principle of tithing, citing scriptures and quoting prophets about the need to pay tithing, but they had no firsthand testimony of the blessings that come from paying tithing. Many of them saw their parents pay tithing, but they themselves had neither earned a paycheck nor felt the good feelings of giving 10 percent to the Lord. They were missing the feeling that comes from fulfilling that commandment of the Lord and supporting His Church.
>
> I am afraid that young people who have not had the opportunity of working hard and paying tithing will have a difficult time paying their tithing and fast offerings and doing the things that those of us who grew up while holding a job and working hard learned to do.
>
> I'm especially convinced, based on what I've observed, that having a job is one of the best ways possible to prepare for the rigors of serving missions. I guarantee you will be a better missionary if you have experienced the success of working a job satisfactorily than if you have never held down a job. Jobs teach many kinds of skills—especially the ability to work hard and work effectively.[7]

A couple of years ago, we ate breakfast with one of our old college professors while we were on a speaking assignment at BYU–Idaho. This great man had served as a mission president several years earlier in the Midwest, so we asked him about the work ethic of his missionaries. He responded, "I would kneel down in front of the transfer board and just pray and plead that the Lord would send me some missionaries who knew how to work. I didn't even care if they had testimonies. I would rather have a missionary who knew how to work and didn't have a testimony—we could deal with that—than a missionary who had a testimony but did not know how to work." What tremendous insight from a mission president! And what a sad commentary on the consequences of the pampered generation. Elder F. David Stanley, a former mission president, said one of the saddest events for a mission president to observe is "elders and sisters coming into the mission field not having learned how to work."[8]

Another returned mission president related to us, "When I received the information about the missionaries coming to our mission, I would always look to see where they were from. When I learned that I had a missionary coming from Idaho, I would let out a cheer, because I knew we had a missionary who could work!" Unfortunately, not all of us are from Idaho. Furthermore, not all of us have farms where we can teach our children the value of hard work. How can today's urban parents teach their children to work as hard as those who grew up on the potato farms of Idaho? President Spencer W. Kimball answered that question when he declared,

> The idle generation! Hours each day and nothing to do. . . . We want you parents to create work for your children. . . . "What can we do?" they ask again. Do the shopping, work in the hospital, help the neighbors and the church custodian, wash dishes, vacuum the floors, make the beds, get the meals, learn to sew. Read good books . . . clean the house, press your clothes, rake the leaves, shovel the snow, peddle papers. . . . Lawmakers in their overeagerness to protect the child have legislated until the pendulum has swung to the other extreme. But no law prohibits most work suggested above, and parents can make work.[9]

Just because many of us live in urban areas does not mean that our children can't learn how to work. There are myriad opportunities and we don't have to look far to find them. Don't wait for the Church to teach your children how to work or to provide opportunities for work. Recently, one of us sat in a ward council meeting where a father pled for the ward to create service opportunities so that his children could serve and help. Why wait for the ward? Why not take the initiative and bring your children over to an elderly neighbor's home and get busy? Why not take a meal to a family in your ward, or do some yard work for someone who needs help? Why wait for our ward leaders to tell us what we already know? Bishop H. David Burton taught, "One of parents' most important responsibilities is to teach their children to work. Even young children can begin to experience the benefits of working when they are involved in household chores and in service to others. Wise parents will work alongside their children, will provide frequent praise, and will make sure no task is overwhelming."[10]

Even if it means sneaking into your local meetinghouse with your family and cleaning it from top to bottom, you don't have to look far to render service. There is so much good that can be done. We recommend that you turn off the television, hide the remote control, power down the computer, confiscate the iPhones, and unplug the Xbox. Load up the family and take them on a search-and-rescue mission in your neighborhood. We promise, there is much work and service that could be provided. We also promise that your family will not forget the experience!

WORK AND CONVERSION

President Harold B. Lee emphatically stated, "The most important responsibility that we, as members of the Church of Jesus Christ, have is to see that we are converted to the truthfulness of the gospel."[11] Parents must assume the vital charge to help their children become converted. What does it take to become converted to the gospel? It certainly takes desire, study, and prayer. President Lee said, "We say to our people whom we teach, 'Now, you ask the Lord. Study, work, and pray.' This is the process by which people are brought into the Church, and it is the same way that from the beginning the honest in heart everywhere have been brought into the Church."[12]

To become converted entails scripture study, reading the words of our modern-day prophets and apostles, praying, fasting, and serving. In John 7:17, Jesus taught His disciples, "If any man will do his will, he shall know of the doctrine, whether it be of God, or whether I speak of myself." Therefore, to become converted also requires living gospel principles. For example, people cannot know the principle of tithing is true until they actually pay tithing. Likewise, a youth cannot know Thomas S. Monson is a true prophet until he or she reads his teachings and then follows them. Furthermore, true conversion implies serving others and caring for them. In order for conversion to occur, the individual must be clean from the sins of the world. To be clean, a person must repent and keep the commandments. One who is converted to the gospel will also be willing to share it with others. True conversion takes time, energy, sacrifice, desire, and work.

Elder D. Todd Christofferson explained in detail what kind of study would be required to become converted to the gospel of Jesus Christ. As you read Elder Christofferson's statement, think of the time, effort, and focus that are required to become converted. He declared,

> For the gospel to be written in your heart, you need to know what it is and grow to understand it more fully. That means you will study it. . . . I see you sometimes reading a few verses, stopping to ponder them, carefully reading the verses again, and as you think about what they mean, praying for understanding, asking questions in your mind, waiting for spiritual impressions, and writing down the impressions and insights that come so you can remember and learn more. Studying in this way, you may not read a lot of chapters or verses in a half hour, but you will be giving place in your heart for the word of God, and He will be speaking to you.[13]

Indeed, learning the gospel is a sacrifice. It takes work! No one ever became converted sitting on their sofa, watching television and eating chips and salsa. There is a price to pay to become converted. Will our youth be willing to ante up? The scriptures use words like *seek, ask,* and *knock* (Matthew 7:7) in order to receive answers to our prayers. In Doctrine and Covenants 88:63, the Lord promised, "Draw near unto me and I will draw near unto you; seek me diligently and ye shall find me; ask, and ye shall receive; knock, and it shall be opened unto you." Seeking, knocking, and asking require work and investment. To gain a testimony and become converted to the gospel will requiring studying, pondering, praying, and practicing. Bubble-wrapped children will have a difficult time expending this kind of effort to a cause, especially if there is no need for God in their high-tech, cushy world.

How will a young man or a young woman become converted if they do not understand and have not lived these principles of work, effort, and sacrifice? Simply put, they won't. A number of years ago, we had the opportunity to ask a stake president about his opinion on getting our youth deeply converted. We expected him to talk about scripture study or prayer, or perhaps even going on exchanges with the missionaries. It surprised us when this stake president began to discuss the principle of work. He related to us that too many of our youth don't know how to work hard, and that there is a direct correlation between working hard and becoming converted to the gospel. He also told us that becoming converted takes just as much time and effort as getting good grades, being a successful violinist, or starring on the high school football team. Not long after that conversation, the stake president's returned missionary son shared this with us:

> Another problem my dad said that limits and hinders conversion among our youth is the growing trend of teenagers not knowing how to work for something. My dad meant this in a very temporal sense. Many youth no longer have jobs during the summer. They don't understand the concept of service (except maybe in organized service projects) and have no concept of sacrifice. My dad attributes this problem to the affluence of the parents. Teenagers don't work today because they don't have to. Their parents make a lot of money and give them whatever they want and need. I know quite a few kids at BYU and on my mission that didn't know how to work at all. They never had to before their missions. I don't remember my dad ever having deep gospel conversations with me while we were working, but what I do remember is that he made sure me and my brothers always had summer jobs, always worked in the yard together every Saturday morning, and always attended every ward service project. Therefore, once I arrived in the mission field, the concept of *work* was never difficult for me to grasp because I had worked for things my entire life. I mean this not only in the sense of physical work as I knocked on doors over nine hours a day in the 120 degree Arizona summer heat, but also work in the sense that I wanted to learn the gospel better. I realized I would have to put forth great effort to do so or it just wouldn't happen.

As we have pondered the words of this inspired priesthood leader and his son, we know they are both right. Teaching your children the value of working hard is not merely so they will become successful contributors of society; it is so that they will become effective builders and protectors of God's kingdom. In order to fulfill that responsibility, they must know how to work!

PRACTICAL APPLICATION

- As a family, study 2 Nephi 5:6–17 and identify the principles of work, industry, prosperity, and success.

- In a family home evening, have one of your children teach "Work and Self-Reliance" from *For the Strength of Youth* (40–41).
- Have assigned chores for your children. Help them understand the principle of work and the happiness that come from a job well done. Resist the temptation to pay your children for helping around the house. There should be chores that children do because they are part of the family. Though there could be other chores that they could be paid for.
- Make sure that your teenagers have a part-time job working for someone besides you.
- Have the missionaries over for dinner and have them share with your children the amount of work that goes into each day. Allow them to share the joys of a hard day's work.

SUPPLEMENTAL RESOURCES

1. H. David Burton, "The Blessing of Work," *Ensign*, December 2009.

2. F. David Stanley, "The Principle of Work," *Ensign*, May 1993.

3. Neal A. Maxwell, "Put Your Shoulder to the Wheel," *Ensign*, May 1998.

4. *For the Strength of Youth*, "Work and Self-Reliance"; https://www. lds.org/youth/for-the-strength-of-youth/work-and-self-reliance?; lang=eng.

5. The Mormon Channel, "A Work in Progress"; http://www. mormonchannel.org/youth-videos?v=1463159448001.

6. The Mormon Channel, *Gospel Solutions for Families,* "Teaching Your Children Values," Part 1—Episode 32, http://www.mormonchannel.org/gospel-solutions-for-families/32; Part 2—Episode 33, http://www.mormonchannel.org/gospel-solutions-for-families/33.

REFERENCES

1. J. Reuben Clark Jr., in Conference Report, April 1933, 103.

2. Ezra Taft Benson, *The Teachings of Ezra Taft Benson* (Salt Lake City: Deseret Book, 1988), 200.

3. As cited in Madaline Levine, *The Price of Privilege* (New York: Harper Collins Publishers, 2006), 77.

4. Charles J. Sykes, *50 Rules Kids Won't Learn in School* (New York: St. Martin's Press, 2007), 2.

5. Gene R. Cook, *Raising Up a Family to the Lord* (Salt Lake City: Deseret Book, 1993), 226.

6. Joe J. Christensen, *One Step at a Time: Building a Better Marriage, Family, and You* (Salt Lake: Deseret Book, 1996), 79.

7. Stephen B. Oveson, "Good Work," *New Era*, January 2007, 37.

8. F. David Stanley, "The Principle of Work," *Ensign*, May 1993.

9. Spencer W. Kimball, *The Teachings of Spencer W. Kimball*, ed. Edward L. Kimball (Salt Lake: Bookcraft, 1982), 360–61.

10. H. David Burton, "The Blessings of Work," *Ensign*, December 2009, 44.

11. Harold B. Lee, *Stand Ye in Holy Places* (Salt Lake City: Deseret Book, 1974), 90.

12. Harold B. Lee, *The Teachings of Harold B. Lee* (Salt Lake City: Bookcraft, 1996), 136.

13. D. Todd Christofferson, in Conference Report, April 2004, 9–10.

CHAPTER 9
PHYSICAL HEALTH
AND APPEARANCE

"There should be an eagerness and a desire to serve the Lord as His ambassadors to the world. And there must be health and strength, both physical and mental, for the work is demanding, the hours are long, and the stress can be heavy."[1]

—Gordon B. Hinckley

SERVING A MISSION isn't like taking a trip to Disneyland. We would be the first to say that we had great fun on our missions, but every day was long, taxing, and tiring. A good missionary will spend twelve to fifteen hours a day in the Lord's service. Without question or doubt, missionary work is physically demanding, emotionally challenging, and spiritually taxing. That is why, in the *Church Handbook of Instructions*, bishops and stake presidents are strongly counseled to only recommend young men and women for missions who are physically, mentally, and emotionally able to serve.

President Gordon B. Hinckley commented on the heavy demands of missionary work when he said,

This work is rigorous. It demands strength and vitality. It demands mental sharpness and capacity. . . . Missionary work is not a rite of passage in the

Church. It is a call extended by the President of the Church to those who are worthy and able to accomplish it. . . . Good physical and mental health is vital. . . . There are parents who say, "If only we can get Johnny on a mission, then the Lord will bless him with health." It seems not to work out that way. Rather, whatever ailment or physical or mental shortcoming a missionary has when he comes into the field only becomes aggravated under the stress of the work. . . . Permit me to emphasize that we need missionaries, but they must be capable of doing the work.[2]

Missionaries who have physical, mental, and emotional challenges not only have their own issues to deal with, but they also limit what their companions are able to do. For example, if a missionary is significantly overweight, the two may not be able to climb hills, walk far distances, ride bikes, or work long stretches of time without resting. Therefore, such missionaries not only compromise their own mission, but they also negatively impact their companion's ability to serve. So it is in the best interest of missionaries to arrive at the MTC in top physical, emotional, and spiritual condition.

PHYSICAL HEALTH

For those interested in embarking on a mission, they must be ready to serve God with all of their "heart, might, mind and strength" (D&C 4:2). Serving in this manner will require all that a missionary can give—especially physically. Though every mission is different, rest assured that wherever your children serve, the mission will be physically demanding. Most missionaries work long days, longer than most are used to. They wake up early and go to bed late. They must walk, bike, and travel long distances and be socially engaged with people all day. Surprisingly, even teaching discussions can be strenuous because of the mental and spiritual exertion that is required. Of course, many missionaries must also exercise intellectual strength and focus to learn and master a foreign language. Because of these demands, most missionaries don't have much difficulty falling asleep at night. Though there are a plethora of things a missionary could do to prepare physically, we wish to emphasize just four: exercise, hygiene, dress, and nutrition.

Exercise

In order to help prepare your son or daughter for missionary work, a good exercise program should become part of the daily regimen. We recommend that all potential missionaries spend some time stretching, improving their strength, and increasing their stamina. Cardiovascular exercise is a powerful tool for strengthening the heart and decreasing stress. Prospective missionaries would do well to start biking, jogging, walking, or swimming to improve their cardiovascular strength and endurance.

Prior to their missions, many youth have engaged in sports, dance, or other activities that have helped them stay physically fit. However, after they graduate from high school, they are often not as physically active as they were as teens, so they need to be more intentional about staying in good shape. Those missionaries who enter the field in great physical condition will more readily be able to bring to pass much good as the Lord's instruments. They will be "workhorses" for their mission presidents and bless many as they tirelessly give the Lord all that they have.

A middle-aged man recently shared one of his greatest regrets from his missionary service. Prior to his mission, he had injured his knee playing sports but was cleared to serve as a missionary. However, the daily grind of biking and walking long distances took its toll on his knee. He opted to not have knee surgery; his doctor felt that physical therapy could help keep him in the mission field. Though this was wonderful news for the missionary, attending physical therapy sessions for his knee greatly hindered the missionary work in his area. His companion eventually became resentful because several days a week they spent an hour or more with a physical therapist instead of doing the work. The healthier the missionary, the greater the contribution to the work will be.

There are several things parents can do to ensure that their future missionaries will be physically fit and prepared to serve as missionaries:

- Teach your son or daughter to begin each day with a healthy regimen of cardiovascular exercise.
- Teach your children the value of going to bed early and waking up early.
- Make sure any of your future missionary's physical problems, such as injuries or illnesses, are taken care of well before his or her time to serve.

Hygiene and Cleanliness

It is the duty of every missionary to look, act, and even *smell* like an ambassador of Jesus Christ. People will judge the Church by the way missionaries appear and how they conduct themselves. Every single missionary should shower with soap daily (if not twice daily), regularly wash his or her hair and comb it, use deodorant, and be clean-shaven. As a health precaution, missionaries should also wash their hands frequently.

One of us remembers a missionary who served in an area where he once lived. The missionary rarely showered, and when he did he never used soap. This was in Texas where the temperatures are high and the humidity is even higher. You could always smell this missionary before he and his companion came around the corner! Few members felt that they could trust such a missionary with their nonmember friends because it would have been embarrassing to introduce him to anyone. Besides losing the trust of the members, this missionary's companion perhaps suffered more than anyone else. It was an extremely frustrating companionship for him, to say the least. Parents, take the time to help your children understand the importance of good hygiene and teach them how to properly care for themselves before they leave home. They should also know how to do certain tasks like iron clothing, sew a button, and shine shoes.

Another area of hygiene would include living quarters. Missionary apartments are notorious for being messy and cluttered. Often, elders and sisters have learned to tolerate filth and disorder. Perhaps their parents never taught them how to do a dish, vacuum a rug, make a bed, mop a floor, or clean a toilet. On the other hand, we have learned that there are individuals who simply do not value cleanliness and order, regardless of what their parents taught them. These individuals simply don't care if their apartment is clean or messy.

Parents, if your children do not have cleanliness skills now, the time has come to prepare them. It is *not* the duty of mission presidents or companions to clean up after their fellow missionaries. Most likely, your son or daughter will see the value and appreciate the Spirit that accompanies a clean apartment. Teach your children the basics of good housekeeping. Be sure they know how to make a bed, do the dishes, and take out the garbage. A missionary apartment should be a sanctuary where missionaries can rest after a long day, find peace, and feel the Spirit. It should be a place where they can receive revelation as they plan out their next day or decide how to resolve the concerns of their investigators. Their apartment should be a refuge and a haven, not a place that should be condemned by the health department!

There are several things parents can do to ensure that their future missionaries develop good hygiene:

- Teach your children the importance of shaving, shampooing, and showering at least daily. Sometimes teenagers feel that they don't need to take a daily shower, but they do.
- Model the principle that "cleanliness is next to godliness." Teach your children how to properly clean a room, a toilet, a tub, a car, and anything else that you can think of. Having daily chores will help your children be more readily prepared in these areas.
- When teaching your children about cleanliness and hygiene, use the temple as an object lesson. The interior and the exterior of the temple can teach us many things about how we should keep our homes and ourselves.

Dress and Appearance

Because missionaries represent the Savior, they should be groomed well and dressed sharply. People are often attracted to the Church because of the clean-cut appearance of missionaries. The *Missionary Handbook* states, "Your appearance is often the first message others receive, and it should support what you say. Therefore, wear conservative, professional clothing that is consistent with your sacred calling. . . . Never allow your appearance or your behavior to draw attention away from your message or your calling."[3]

For years, elders have been admonished to wear conservative-colored suits, shoes, and socks. Moreover, white shirts and simple ties have been the standard missionary attire for years. Elders have also been directed to keep their hair short and evenly tapered. They are to avoid extreme or faddish hairstyles, including spiked, permed, or bleached hair.[4]

We have attended numerous wards where priesthood leaders have expected the young men who administer the sacrament to look and act like missionaries. Or, in other words, these young men did not wait until they were eighteen or nineteen years old to begin dressing like disciples of

Jesus Christ. Their missionary preparation began when they were twelve as they wore the proper priesthood attire to officiate in ordinances. Not surprisingly, in these wards, most of the young men seemed to be well prepared for their missions when they came of age. The percentage of missionaries who served from such wards seems higher when compared to those wards that have lower standards.

We have also attended wards were there were minimal standards required to prepare, bless, and pass the sacrament. Some of the young men we have seen performing the ordinance have worn colored shirts and their hair has been longer, stringier, bushier, or more colorful than a missionary's hair should be. We have wondered why such appearances are tolerated, or even allowed, by parents or leaders. Why not begin expecting our young men to look like missionaries from the moment they turn twelve, or even earlier? Why do we have eighteen-year-old young men at the sacrament table who look like they are heading to a rock concert instead of officiating in priesthood ordinances?

Once again, our informal observation is that families and wards that treat the ordinances casually end up having their priesthood force become casualties. The earlier our young men embrace the standards that they will be expected to live by as missionaries, the more likely they are to be ready to serve and become faithful and obedient sons of God.

Sister missionaries also have been given standards to live by. They too represent the Savior and His teachings. Sister missionaries are expected to wear modest clothing that's not too tight or too loose, revealing in anyway, drawing attention to any part of their bodies, or casual or sloppy. Sister missionaries are to wear skirts, blouses, and jackets that fit well and are conservative in color and appearance. Like the elders, the sisters should also have hairstyles that do not call attention to themselves.

Young women can begin preparing for their missions by dressing modestly. This begins as a teenager as they follow the counsel in *For the Strength of Youth*. Like the young men, girls can begin in their younger years to dress more conservatively. They shouldn't wear immodest bathing suits, short-shorts, or tight-fitting shirts. Again, like the young men, they don't need to wait until they are missionaries to dress like disciples of Jesus Christ.

There are several things parents can do to ensure that their future missionaries develop good dress and grooming habits:

- Parents have to set the example of how to dress appropriately. Children can smell hypocrites from miles away. If an LDS mother wears short-shorts or bikinis, it'll be quite difficult to convince her mission-bound daughter that she needs to dress modestly.

- Parents, make sure your sons have white shirts and ties to wear to Church on Sunday. Discuss the importance of keeping their hair cut at a certain length so they can be dignified and serve in their priesthood duties. Elder Jeffrey R. Holland taught, "May I suggest that wherever possible a white shirt be worn by the deacons, teachers, and priests who handle the sacrament. For sacred ordinances in the Church we often use ceremonial clothing, and a white shirt could be seen as a gentle reminder of the white clothing you wore in the baptismal font and an anticipation of the white shirt you will soon wear into the temple and onto your missions."[5]

- Help your children understand that people will judge the Church by the image they portray. A clean-cut image goes a long way in furthering the Lord's work.

Nutrition

Depending where your son or daughter serves will also determine, to a large degree, what their diet will be. We have had children who have served in Latin American countries and ate beans and rice with every meal, and we have also had children who served in the United States and ate no differently than they did at home. In some locations, missionaries may eat their evening meals with Church members. In others, missionaries may be required to make every meal they eat.

Nevertheless, missionaries will need proper fuel so their bodies will function at the highest level. This means eliminating junk foods, carbonated drinks, and other substances that provide short energy spurts rather than long periods of strength and endurance. Besides all of that, missionaries don't have time to visit the dentist while on their missions.

Parents, it would be worthwhile to sit down with your children and teach them how to make nutritious meals for minimal costs. Most young men and women can be taught how to prepare eggs, oatmeal, pancakes, soups, sandwiches, salads, and pastas. Make sure you teach your children how to make a variety of meals that they won't get bored with. We know of missionaries who ate macaroni and cheese each night to save money, but that wasn't the best idea for their health.

There are several things parents can do to ensure that their future missionaries will be able to take care of themselves nutritionally:

- Teach your children to drink plenty of water to stay hydrated. Depending on the area they serve in, six to twelve glasses a day would be appropriate.
- Teach your children the value of eating five to seven fruits or vegetables daily. They should also include protein such as nuts, beans, cheese, eggs, fish, poultry, and meat.
- Teach your children to live the Word of Wisdom. If they are going to commit investigators to live that commandment, then they should live it too. To drive this point home, read Doctrine and Covenants 89:18–21 and discuss the promises the Lord gives to those who follow His commandments regarding nutrition.

The healthier a young man or woman is physically, the more he or she will be able to accomplish as a missionary. When missionaries look and act like the Lord's disciples, their ability to teach and influence others becomes powerful. As missionaries obey these directives, the greatest blessing will be the Holy Ghost who attends them, protects them, and guides them to those who are seeking the truth.

PRACTICAL APPLICATION

- Parents, share with your children what you do for exercise and try to find ways to exercise together as a family.
- Teach your children how to make several easy and nutritious meals. Allow them to make meals for the family before they leave on their missions.
- Study together the *Missionary Handbook*, which can be accessed at https://www.lds.org/manual/missionary-handbook?lang=eng. Pages 7–42 focus on a missionary's conduct. This would be appropriate and helpful for young men and young women to begin studying as teenagers.

- Have your children teach a family home evening lesson on proper dress, modesty, and physical appearance. A powerful resource is *For the Strength of Youth,* under the title "Dress and Appearance." There are also many other resources that can be accessed at www.lds.org.
- Make sure your child's physical health concerns have been taken care of professionally before he or she enters the MTC.

SUPPLEMENTAL RESOURCES

1. *Missionary Preparation Student Manual,* "Chapter 11: Physical and Emotional Preparation"; https://www.lds.org/manual/missionary-preparation-student-manual/chapter-11-physical-and-emotional-preparation?lang=eng.

2. "What Are the Physical Fitness Requirements to Serve a Mission?" *New Era,* September 2013; https://www.lds.org/new-era/2013/09/to-the-point/what-are-the-physical-fitness-requirements-to-serve-a-mission?lang=eng.

3. "President Monson: Missionary Work"; https://www.lds.org/prophets-and-apostles/unto-all-the-world/prepare-to-be-a-missionary?lang=eng.

REFERENCES

1. Gordon B. Hinckley, "Missionary Service," *First Worldwide Leadership Training Meeting,* January 2003, 17–18; as cited in the *Missionary Preparation Student Manual,* 89.

2. Ibid.

3. *Missionary Handbook* (Salt Lake City: The Church of Jesus Christ of Latter-day Saints, 2006), 10.

4. See *Missionary Handbook* (Salt Lake City: The Church of Jesus Christ of Latter-day Saints, 2006), 11.

5. Jeffrey R. Holland, "This Do in Remembrance of Me," *Ensign,* November 1995.

CHAPTER 10
EMOTIONAL HEALTH
AND RESILIENCY

"Missionary service is emotionally demanding. . . . There will be days of rejection and disappointment. Learn now about your emotional limits, and learn how to control your emotions under the circumstances you will face as a missionary."[1]

—L. Tom Perry

SOME OF THE best missionaries in recorded history have struggled with the stresses and strains a mission can bring. Ammon and his brethren, who "suffer[ed] much, both in body and in mind, such as hunger, thirst and fatigue, and also much labor in the spirit" (Alma 17:5). It appears that there were times that at some points even these stalwart missionaries wanted to pack it up and head home. For example, further in it reads, "Now when our hearts were depressed, and we were about to turn back, behold, the Lord comforted us, and said: Go amongst thy brethren, the Lamanites, and bear with patience thine afflictions, and I will give unto you success" (Alma 26:27).[2]

President Gordon B. Hinckley, another legendary missionary, also wanted to pack up and go home shortly after his mission began. Only a few weeks in, President Hinckley was discouraged and wrote his father a letter, in which he explained that the mission was a waste of his time and his father's money. His father wrote back, "Dear Gordon, I have your recent letter. I have only one suggestion: forget yourself and go to work." President Hinckley further explained that earlier that morning while studying the scriptures, he read, "Whosoever will save his life shall lose it; but whosoever shall lose his life for my sake and the gospel's, the same shall save it" (Mark 8:35). With the penetrating words of his father and the perfectly timed verse from the New Testament, President Hinckley vowed that he would forget himself and go to work. He did so and served as a powerful missionary in Great Britain.[3]

All missionaries will have their fair share of discouragement as they serve in their assigned fields of labor. How they handle the emotional challenges and disappointments that missions are sure to bring will largely determine how successfully they will serve, and how happy they will be. Parents can help their children prepare for missions by assessing their resiliency and teaching them how to manage disappointment, challenges, trials, fears, and frustrations. Our missionary force certainly needs to be both physically and emotionally tough.

HOME IS THE LABORATORY OF EMOTIONAL HEALTH

Recently, one of us talked with a concerned father and his young daughter. This particular young woman was completing her missionary application. Her father described her as a loner who rarely came out of her bedroom. She appeared depressed and unmotivated and had been this way for a large portion of her teenage years.

When asked if she was worried, nervous, and concerned about serving a mission, she mumbled, "Sure." When the father was asked about his daughter's anxiety and readiness to serve, he said, "Well, I told her she should at least try." Instead of sending her out into the mission field, her counselor recommended that she go to college for a year. After that, depending on how it worked out, she could consider a mission. That proved to be wise counsel. Sending a missionary with emotional challenges into the field with the hopes that their anxiety, depression, anger, or other emotional issues will simply disappear as they engage in missionary work is certainly not an appropriate "plan of attack."

Remember President Hinckley's admonition: "Whatever ailment or physical or mental shortcoming a missionary has when he comes into the field only becomes aggravated under the stress of the work."[4] President Hinckley urged parents to never assume that a mission will alleviate physical and emotional challenges. Instead, children should be able to manage their problems before they take on the burdens of missionary service, for a mission will not make emotional problems and mood disorders disappear; instead, it will exacerbate them.

EARLY RETURNED MISSIONARIES

Elder L. Tom Perry taught, "Missionary service is emotionally demanding. Your support system is going to be withdrawn from you as you leave home and go out into the world. . . . There will be days of rejection and disappointment. Learn now about your emotional limits, and learn how to control your emotions under the circumstances you will face as a missionary."[5] In reality, emotional preparedness may be more critical to a missionary's success than almost any other area of preparation. We have yet to counsel with an ERM—early returned missionary—who came home prematurely because he or she couldn't sew on a button or had failed to memorize a scripture.

A recent study conducted by researchers at Utah Valley University found that when they surveyed ERMs about why they returned home early, about thirty-six percent reported having debilitating mental health issues. The following graphic reveals the top reasons missionaries return home before their missions are complete.

Jonathan Sandberg, a marriage and family therapist who often works with ERMs, declared, "Anxiety and depression and obsessive-compulsive disorder are the three main reasons we are seeing people coming home, and it's the inability to handle new stressors." And moreover, thirty-eight percent of ERMs said that stress was a contributing factor to their coming home from their missions prematurely.[6] And thirty-four percent

Reasons for early returns
Top reasons why 348 men and women returned home early from their LDS missions.

34% Physical health issues

36% Mental health issues

12%

11% Unresolved transgression

7% Other

Disobedience to mission rules

Source: Kristine J. Doty, "Understanding and Assisting Early Returning Missionaries," Utah Valley University
DESERET NEWS GRAPHIC

reported physical issues were the cause of them coming home early (see graphic). However, in our clinical practices, we have learned that many of those physical issues, such as headaches, back pain, insomnia, dizziness, stomach problems, and even sore throats are not *always* the root of the problem. The core issues that often serve as a catalyst for these physical symptoms turn out to be anxiety, stress, or depression.

As one ERM said, rather the mission being the best two years, it turned out to be the worst three months. The result, as many Church leaders, parents, and ERMs can attest, is a stigma that is difficult to face in our LDS culture. For a variety of reasons, many youth have great difficulty emotionally coping with daily stresses. They may battle depression or anxiety. They may have limited social growth because of excessive computer gaming or family isolation. Perhaps they were never expected to do much in their homes.

As they approach mission age, they are faced with an uncomfortable dilemma. On the one hand, if they should delay or chose not to serve, they perceive that they'll face the constant scrutiny of Church leaders, family, and nosy ward members, wanting to know why they haven't left on their missions. Though this pressure may be more *perceived* than actual, it is their reality, and they feel it strongly.

On the other hand, the emotional rigors of working an eighteen-hour day in the mission field can quickly expose and aggravate poor mental balance. Whether the reaction is diagnosed as emotional or physical with psychological roots, the result is the same, that being most missionaries are unable to continue.

The other part of the dilemma is having missionaries come home prematurely. As most can attest, coming home as an ERM is extremely painful. We've watched as they cope with this "failure" in a variety of ways. Sometimes they take Sunday jobs so they don't have to be in church. Others go off to YSA wards yet never really attend. Or perhaps they go off to school somewhere—no one really knows where exactly. Sometimes they live with family members. Others lose their passion for the gospel and stop coming to Church.

In most cases, their self-worth has been shattered and they feel ashamed, now labeled as a missionary who "couldn't cut it." It would have been so much better for these individuals to have delayed their missions until they were more prepared emotionally or found other avenues where they could serve and make a difference.

We have all known someone who may not have been too strongly prepared to serve yet blossomed as a missionary. It happens. Many have returned from missions changed, becoming confident and mature. Testimonies have been drastically strengthened, conversions have taken place, and lives have simply been renovated. However, for every prospective missionary who successfully overcomes great shyness or anxiety or low self-worth and serves successfully, there are increasing amounts who are crumbling emotionally due to improper preparation or treatment prior to their decision to serve. Our hope is that we can help provide parents with the necessary tools so that their young men and women don't return home prematurely from the mission field. The following checklist is a great start:

EMOTIONAL CHECKLIST

Let's begin with a quick emotional assessment. There is nothing greatly scientific about these questions, but we feel this is a good beginning point for evaluating a potential missionary's resiliency. Have the prospective missionary circle the number that he or she believes most others would select to describe him or her.

How well would others say . . .	Well				Poor
I act when I am feeling angry?	5	4	3	2	1
I react when others around me are angry?	5	4	3	2	1
I react to disappointment and failure?	5	4	3	2	1
I let go of disappointments?	5	4	3	2	1
I react to being criticized?	5	4	3	2	1
I react when I am discouraged?	5	4	3	2	1
I respond to stressful situations?	5	4	3	2	1
I make friends?	5	4	3	2	1
I can talk to people I don't know?	5	4	3	2	1
I express what I need?	5	4	3	2	1
I make decisions and solve problems?	5	4	3	2	1
I adapt to new situations?	5	4	3	2	1
I react when others around me are stressed?	5	4	3	2	1

Total up the circled responses to determine an overall score.

13–25: Emotionally brittle. Scores in this range suggest an inability to function well in stressful situations. Individuals who are emotionally brittle react poorly to criticism and the feedback of others. This makes it difficult for them to interact well with strangers and in new situations because they don't know what to expect. They might take a long time to recover from embarrassing or stressful encounters with others. Potential missionaries who are emotionally brittle tend to have ongoing conflicts with companions and find it hard to be motivated to work hard when they are emotionally down. Those who score in this category could use some counseling prior to their missions, or should read some good books that will help them shore up their emotional strength.

26–35: Areas of concern. Scores in this range suggest that there are some major areas that need to be addressed. Look at the lowest categories. Potential missionaries with these scores have learned to build up areas of strength to compensate for weaker ones. Yet, there are still areas that could cause a mission to unravel if not addressed.

36–45: Awareness. These scores suggest there is enough strength to probably compensate for the weaker areas. These strengths enable missionaries to function well while emotional growth is occurring. Such strengths are often spiritual gifts that more than compensate for other, less developed areas.

46–65: Resiliency. The higher the scores here, the more able an individual is to weather the stress of new and difficult situations. They bounce back quickly from disappointment and are less likely to dwell on failure. They are also less likely to take criticism personally while still learning from helpful feedback. These kinds of missionaries will be influential in helping other missionaries be strong.

Performing an honest assessment of the emotional strength of future missionaries requires us to look objectively at their resiliency. True, they are still young and a mission will bring a level of maturity that they likely won't get any other way. On the other hand, we must clearly address the real deficits and not set missionaries up to potentially fail. Recently, one of us saw an eighteen-year-old girl in his office. She was smart and articulate, yet extremely depressed. She was overly focused on maintaining her high GPA. She also worried excessively about her spiritual standing and was constantly laden with guilt about the smallest of sins. At this juncture, she was entertaining suicidal thoughts.

She was clearly clinically depressed. It was suggested to her father that she should be on some medication, at least for a short period of time while we worked on the underlying issues. Weeks later, the girl returned, still depressed and stressing over her graduation. She reported that her father did not like the idea of using medication and had refused to take her to a doctor. After visiting again with her father, he finally (reluctantly) agreed to let her try "the meds."

Several weeks later, this young woman returned. She was much brighter, optimistic, and managing her depression much better. With the proper medication, she began feeling well and her symptoms were drastically alleviated. At that point in counseling, we were then able to deal with some of her obsessive habits and helped her make some lasting changes.

Loving parents and concerned Church leaders, anxious to see their youth get out on missions, can unintentionally have blind spots when it comes to emotional weaknesses. They may have preconceived ideas about a child "just needing to grow up," or feelings about medication or professional help. Youth can say that they are just fine and have a lack of insight into their own emotional brittleness. And yet, these problems will generally fester and finally surface under the pressure of a mission. These missionaries could have difficult companions or months with few teaching prospects. They could work long days with little results. They will be cut off from their music, computers, TV, phones, and any other ways they used to cope with stress and conflict. Even when they are feeling down, they will have to put on their game face and interact, cheer up others, and make a difference. Moreover, they will have to do all of this without the help of a parent who can talk them off the ledge or a sibling who knows when to give them space. Frankly, they will have to forget about themselves and go to work. They need to develop a level of emotional resiliency that enables them to ride through some rough seas without capsizing. And they must be able to do this while they are outside their comfort zone.

EMOTIONS

So how do we build emotional resiliency in our children? As parents, we first have to teach them to read their emotional reactions.

Recently, I (Kevin) had a client whom I asked: "Are your emotions good are bad?"

She looked at me for a long while, and then shook her head. "I don't know," she replied.

I went on to ask her about her the fuel gauge on her car, which tells her how much gas is in the tank.

"Is your fuel gauge good or bad?" I asked.

She smiled and said, "I guess it's not either one. It just tells me how much gas I have."

And she was right. Her gauge wasn't good or bad. It just provided information about her car. She could choose to ignore the information or act on it. Her decision was on her—but that decision would have consequences. We need our youth to understand that their emotions—anger, sadness, fear, and stress—aren't good or bad. They simply provide valuable information about how our body is reacting to the world and people around us. If we ignore our emotional gauges, we place ourselves in peril. We need to respond and make adjustments.

For instance, when our youth report being depressed, they need to figure out what the emotions in their bodies are trying to tell them. Their fuel gauges might be telling them they can't live on four hours of sleep a night. Or the gauges might be saying that they are grieving over not making the drill team. They might also need to know that suicidal thoughts are not normal and that professional counseling might help them see the source of the thoughts and learn coping skills.

WHAT PARENTS CAN DO TO RAISE RESILIENT CHILDREN

Show affection, verbally and physically. Learn to speak your child's love language. Love them in ways that are unique to them. Parents, your children must be regulated. They must have rules and they must be disciplined. Believe it or not, this structure provides children with certainty, consistency, and stability that will help them become much stronger emotionally.

Parents, don't hover over your children as "helicopter parents." You will not be able to be with them in the mission field, so begin now by helping your children become independent from you. Children cannot develop resilience while their parents are holding their hands and feeding them a steady diet of candy-flavored cereals and cheese whiz. Character is developed when there is resistance, not coddling. Character is forged when life is tough, not while floating on a raft in a pool. Let them fight their own battles. Teach them to make their own way.

Teach them how to solve problems and take healthy risks. Help them learn to trust themselves and come up with their own solutions. Reward them with praise when they become independent problem-solvers.

Teach your children how to tolerate discomfort. Let them know that life isn't always a bed of roses and that it's okay to mess up, fail, and start all over again. That's called life. The sooner they learn that lesson, the better off they will be.

Provide your children with increasing responsibility for managing their own lives. And when they fail to be accountable for their decisions, let the consequences occur. Also, when they succeed, praise them and point out their accomplishments.

Help them learn from their mistakes. Teach them that when they fall short, they have actually gained an opportunity to grow and improve.

When possible, encourage your child to live away from home for brief periods of time before the mission field. This may be difficult now that the missionary ages have been lowered, but perhaps there are opportunities—even if they are short periods of time—where prospective missionaries can be away from home long enough to learn to "wash their own clothing, clean their own living areas, prepare food, and be responsible for their own safety and well-being."[7]

President Thomas S. Monson declared, "Life was never intended to consist of a glut of luxury, be an easy course, or filled only with success. There are those games which we lose, those races in which we finish last, and those promotions which never come. Such experiences provide an opportunity for us to show our determination and to rise above disappointment."[8]

PRACTICAL APPLICATION

- Teach your children basic management techniques for stress such as exercising, resting and relaxing, letting go of control, and focusing on gratitude. Parents could purchase the booklet

"Adjusting to Missionary Life" from the distribution center or an LDS bookstore. These could be reviewed in FHE, family council, and other settings.

- Assess your child's emotional strength. Create some role-plays and scenarios that you could walk through to teach coping principles for various situations that could arise in the mission field.

- Make sure your children's emotional concerns have been taken care of before they enter the MTC.

- Begin teaching your children to be emotionally tough at an early age. Provide tools for them to solve their own problems and to be in tune to others who need help.

SUPPLEMENTAL RESOURCES

1. *Missionary Preparation Student Manual*, "Chapter 11: Physical and Emotional Preparation"; https://www.lds.org/manual/missionary-preparation-student-manual/chapter-11-physical-and-emotional-preparation?lang=eng.

2. *Missionary Preparation*, "Physical and Emotional Health"; https://www.lds.org/topics/missionary-preparation/physical-and-emotional-health?lang=eng.

3. *For the Strength of Youth*, "Physical and Emotional Health"; https://www.lds.org/manual/for-the-strength-of-youth/physical-and-emotional-health?lang=eng&query=Missionary+Emotional+Health.

4. LDS Media Library, "Mission Preparation Track 20-1: Gordon B. Hinckley"; https://www.lds.org/media-library/video/2012-12-1230-mission-preparation-track-20-1-gordon-b-hinckley?lang=eng.

5. Robert K. Wagstaff, "Preparing Emotionally for Missionary Service," *Ensign*, March 2011, 23.

REFERENCES

1. L. Tom Perry, "Raising the Bar," *Ensign*, November 2007, 48.

2. Ideas taken from "Adjusting to Missionary Life" (Salt Lake City: The Church of Jesus Christ of Latter-day Saints, 2013), 1–2.

3. Adapted from Gordon B. Hinckley, "Words of the Prophet: Put Your Shoulder to the Wheel," *New Era*, July 2000, 7; see also "Adjusting to Missionary Life" (Salt Lake City: The Church of Jesus Christ of Latter-day Saints, 2013), 2.

4. Gordon B. Hinckley, "Missionary Service," *First Worldwide Leadership Training Meeting*, January 2003, 17–18.

5. L. Tom Perry, "Raising the Bar," *Ensign*, November 2007, 48.

6. Tad Walch, "Many Mormon Missionaries Who Return Home Early Feel Some Failure," *Deseret News*, December 6, 2013; http://www.deseretnews.com/article/865591983/LDS-missionaries-developing-strategies-to-cope-with-stress.html?pg=all.

7. Robert K. Wagstaff, "Preparing Emotionally for Missionary Service," *Ensign*, March 2011, 23.

8. Thomas S. Monson, "Go For It!" *Ensign*, May 1989, 43.

CHAPTER 11
THE POWER OF HEALTHY
COMMUNICATION

"Our communications are at the core of our relationships with others. If we are to return home safely to Heavenly Father, we must develop righteous relationships with His children here in mortality."[1]

—L. Lionel Kendrick

EFFECTIVE COMMUNICATION IS the most basic social skill that a missionary will need to serve successfully. If a missionary has a difficult time communicating, it will be hard to fulfill his or her purpose and calling. The late Stephen R. Covey called communication "the most fundamental and necessary skill in life."[2] When we talk about communication in this chapter, we will not be referring to learning a foreign language—though that is important. Instead, we will be discussing how missionaries can learn to be more Christlike in their communication.

A missionary is essentially communicating during every waking hour of his or her ministry. Even when they aren't talking, they are communicating. The most effective missionaries learn to become skilled communicators. We believe that one of the reasons missionaries grow and mature so quickly is because they are often communicating with people much older than them. In a young man's or young woman's world prior to his or her mission, most conversations occurred with peers and family members. However, once in the field, a missionary is constantly talking to mature adults, among them seasoned members and experienced priesthood leaders. This means that a missionary must elevate his or her game and learn to speak the language of adults, eloquently and fluently.

SOCIAL SKILLS

If missionaries want to gain the trust of ward members, they must be able to communicate in polished and positive ways. They must be confident as they approach others and greet them. Missionaries should look people in the eye and speak to them in positive tones.

Of course, not all communication is verbal. For example, one of us knew a missionary who liked to excessively squeeze when he shook hands with others. He was rebuked several times—quite sharply, we might add—by sisters in the ward who actually were physically hurt by his handshake. Prospective missionaries should learn to shake hands firmly, finding a balance so as not to be too weak and certainly not too strong.

There are verbal issues that must be addressed as a missionary. The following is a true story. We will change the names to protect those involved. Years ago, Elders Clark and Davis served in the Pacific Northwest as missionaries. Elder Clark had been in the area for several months. Prior to Elder Davis's arrival, Elder Clark and his previous companion had spent a significant amount of time building bridges and strengthening relationships with the ward members and stake leaders. They had done such a wonderful job that, in a testimony meeting just a week before Elder Davis arrived, one of the members stated in his testimony that he believed the current missionaries were the best he had ever seen, and he urged all of the members to refer their nonmember friends to these missionaries. Most members of that ward felt the same way. That all changed when Elder Davis came to town. Upon his arrival, a member of the bishopric asked him to speak in Church. Instead of nurturing the delicate member-missionary relationship in his remarks, Elder Davis told his new ward that they all "stunk" at missionary work and that they needed to repent and become more missionary-minded. Elder Clark put his head down and basically wanted to crawl out of the building.

That was it. It was only a sentence or two, but Elder Davis destroyed everything Elder Clark and his previous companion had worked to build. Communication can make or break a missionary and a ward. Obviously, if Elder Davis knew anything about human relations, he would not have been so clumsy and careless in the message. After all, did he really believe that calling the members to repentance would inspire them to do missionary work?

There are many things that parents can do to teach their children to be strong, powerful, and positive communicators. Parents can teach their children while they are young to acquire proper social skills so they can interact with others in healthy ways. Consider the following communication skills:

- *Rapport:* Missionaries call this "building relationships of trust." The greatest rule in building rapport is to be attentive to other people. Find out what their interests are and discover what you have in common. For instance, if you're a missionary and are in someone's home, take notice of what is hanging on the walls, the construction of the home, the plants, the children, and so on. Also find out what people do for work, learn about the cars they drive, and discover their hobbies and where they spend their time. Then build the relationship by asking about some of these areas of interest and see how you can connect with them. While one of us was serving our mission, he met an investigator who loved sports. He explained to him that one of the wards he served in played basketball every morning at 5:30 a.m. He invited him to join, and the man happily did so. Within a matter of months, he and his family joined the Church.

- *Tact:* Effective missionaries are polite. They treat people how they want to be treated. They are kind and delicate in the words they use, never intentionally offending anyone, or saying anything rude or harsh. If an investigator, companion, ward member, or priesthood leader needs correction, a missionary with tact would speak in kind tones to build the person up and inspire improvement. In the previous example with Elder Davis, it's clear that Elder Davis lacked tact. Being tactful is being sensitive and considerate of others. In Alma 38:12, we learn missionaries should be bold but not overbearing. Doctrine and Covenants also provides some powerful training on how missionaries can be tactful. We learn in these verses that the rights of the priesthood are directly connected with the powers of heaven and those powers can only be controlled by righteous living; when we try to cover our sins, gratify our pride or vain ambitions, or exercise control or dominion or compulsion (which is what tactlessness is), the powers of heaven are withdrawn from us; when men have authority, they often exercise unrighteous dominion; the most powerful ways to influence or minister to people include persuasion, long-suffering, gentleness, meekness, love, kindness, and pure knowledge; and when we do need to correct someone, we should show an increase in love afterward (see D&C 121:33–43).

- *Enthusiasm:* Missionaries should be the most hopeful, enthusiastic, faith-filled, and optimistic people on the planet. Chronically sad missionaries aren't paying attention to the Lord's hand in their lives. We believe Christ was enthusiastic. In Matthew 4, Jesus saw Peter and Andrew fishing. He said, "Follow me, and I will make you fishers of men" (Matthew 4:19). We believe that Jesus made that invitation with passion and a smile on His face, as immediately Peter and Andrew left their nets and followed Jesus (Matthew 4:20). Our Savior was full of hope, faith, and optimism. He was sincere and genuine. Likewise, missionaries should learn to be genuinely happy. There is nothing worse than a fake missionary who comes across more like a used car salesman than a disciple of Christ. A missionary's gusto for the Lord's work should be normal, not unusual. Our future missionaries need to learn to let their lights shine, though without blinding people.

- *Meekness and Humility:* In the field, we meet missionaries from every walk of life. Prior to their missions, some accomplished incredible feats in music, sports, academics, and athletics. And some of these missionaries enjoyed telling others about their accomplishments, while others didn't say a word. Then there were those who didn't accomplish much before their missions but made up stories about how incredible their lives were before. One of us served with a "small in stature" missionary companion who talked in every lesson, Church meeting, devotional, and fireside about how incredible of a football player he was in high school. Years later, he found out that the elder never even played. An important social skill is learning to think less of ourselves and more of others. Speaking of Jesus, John the Baptist taught, "He must increase, but I must decrease" (John 3:30). John knew the attention from his followers had to be directed toward Christ, not him. Therefore, missionaries should be meek and humble. As missionaries engage in becoming disciples of Jesus Christ, they will mature to the point where they will think more of others and less of themselves. Members and nonmembers will respect them more if they talk less about themselves and show a genuine interest in them.

- *Politeness and Courtesy:* Missionaries should use good manners and put the needs of companions, investigators, ward members, and priesthood leaders above their own. Such missionaries will say please and thank you to those they interact with. They will send thank-you notes to those who do kind things for them. They will express gratitude openly and publicly to those who have blessed their lives. Polite missionaries greet people on the streets with a smile, wave to those who drive past them, and talk to neighbors and children they meet. When missionaries converse with people, instead of talking about themselves, they should ask people questions to learn more about them. Simply put, missionaries are in tune with the needs of those around them. When someone looks like they need help, missionaries are the first to offer assistance.

- *Listening:* Talking actually is not the most important social skill in missionary work. Listening is. Some have argued that is why the Lord gave us one mouth but two ears! Parents, there is little more important than teaching your children to be good listeners. Missionaries should learn to listen to others in such a way that the person they are listening to feels loved and understood. To practice listening effectively, learn to repeat back in your own words what someone has told you. An effective phrase could be,

"So, what you're telling me is _____?" or perhaps something along the lines of, "It sounds like you're saying that _____." People need to feel that they have been heard and understood. Another critical listening skill is learning to show empathy. *Empathy* is the ability to understand someone's feelings, experiences, and emotions. It is connecting with another individual in such a way that they know you understand them. If a companion or an investigator has a hard day and shares how he or she is feeling, a missionary shows empathy by sharing a similar experience or by saying, "I know how you're feeling." Though this is simple, it can make a huge difference in the lives of others.

SPEAKING WITH THE TONGUE OF ANGELS

If a missionary is not prepared for the challenges of the field or grew up in a family that is critical and negative, he or she may radiate negativity as a missionary. Yes, there are many missionaries who whine, complain, and moan about their lives. Unfortunately, when they share negative feelings with members or nonmembers, their credibility can be diminished rapidly. If we as Latter-day Saints have the greatest message in the world, what will nonmembers think if a missionary is constantly complaining about everything?

The Apostle Paul set a high standard for each of us when he declared, "Let no corrupt communication proceed out of your mouth, but that which is good to the use of edifying, that it may minister grace unto the hearers" (Ephesians 4:29). Therefore, a missionary should only speak about things that can heal and edify. There is no room on a mission for murmuring, backbiting, or criticizing. A missionary will learn to find the good in everyone. Orson F. Whitney said, "The spirit of the gospel is optimistic; it trusts in God and looks on the bright side of things. The opposite or pessimistic spirit drags men down and away from God, looks on the dark side, murmurs, complains, and is slow to yield obedience."[3] Teach your children at an early age to find the good and to become optimistic and hopeful.

Nephi taught that we should speak with the tongue of angels (see 2 Nephi 32:2). What does this mean? We should speak and say those things that an angel would say. Angels bring glad tidings! Therefore, prospective missionaries should learn to give praise, compliments, and positive reinforcement to others. This practice should begin at home. One of us had a child in his family that liked to cut down or "diss" other members of the family. We believe that this is not appropriate behavior. We recognize that this is normal behavior for siblings; however, just because it is normal doesn't mean we have to tolerate it. So what did he do? He read some scriptures, like the ones mentioned previously; he shared his testimony with the child of why it's not okay to do such things to family; and then he employed an intervention. Each time this child was caught verbally cutting down a member of the family, he or she had to write five positive things about that family member. It didn't take long for the bad habit to discontinue.

PASSIVE, AGGRESSIVE, OR ASSERTIVE COMMUNICATION

Perhaps one of the most stressful situations that missionaries face is dealing with conflict. Of course, missionaries will have conflicts with some nonmembers and occasionally with the investigators they teach. However, missionaries could also encounter differences with companions, ward members, and even possibly priesthood leaders. If missionaries handle conflict poorly, their stress levels, anxiety, and depression could escalate. However, if such conflicts are handled appropriately, they will be more able to maintain their emotional health and peace.

Parents can teach their future missionaries about the three main responses to verbal conflict: passive, aggressive, and assertive.

Passive responses in communication are when individuals don't stand up for themselves. They allow others to run right over them. Passive people are afraid to speak up, will agree with others just to keep the peace, and really don't value their own opinions. Passive communication is unhealthy because individuals aren't respecting their own needs or beliefs. Ironically, most people don't respect those who respond to them passively either. Some missionaries may confuse passivity with being meek and humble, or even Christlike—but it's actually not any of those. In reality, they are being dishonest with themselves and others. Nowhere in the scriptures or the teachings of the prophets are we counseled to lie on the ground and let others walk all over us while we practically thank them for doing so. Instead, we learn from the scriptures and our leaders that we should be defenders of the faith, champions for truth and righteousness.

On the other hand, aggressive responses to communication don't value the opinions of others and talk over and interrupt them. When individuals deal with an aggressive person, they are often devastated by the encounter. Aggressive people speak up too often and believe their opinion is the right way. Aggressive communication is unhealthy because it doesn't respect the needs of others. Furthermore, aggressive individuals believe that they are rarely wrong. While passive individuals allow others to make decisions for them, aggressive people reject others' ideas and are inconsiderate of any opinion other than their own. An aggressive approach is the opposite of Christlike behavior, and aggressive missionaries could paint the Church in a bad light.

For example, we are aware of a missionary who served in the United States several years ago. In the area where he served, there was a strong anti-Mormon influence. As he and his companion would ride their bikes, often people would drive up, roll down their windows, and yell vulgarities or make obscene gestures toward the missionaries. This particular missionary, once he had his fill, made the same gestures and shouted the same obscenities right back at them. We are sure that this approach caught the persecutors by surprise. It certainly was the wrong way for a disciple of Jesus Christ to handle such abuse. We cannot imagine Christ or any of His prophets arguing with people and trading an eye for an eye.

Since the phrase *passive-aggressive* is often used, let us mention why that is another unhealthy approach to communication. To be passive-aggressive means individuals are passive in their communication during the conflict; however, they take an aggressive approach once the person who's causing the conflict isn't there. For example, if an angry landlord confronts a missionary, that missionary may respond passively to the accusations of paying his or her rent late. However, once the landlord hangs up the phone or walks away, the missionary speaks in harsh, aggressive tones about the "lame" landlord. So, like the other approaches to conflict that we have mentioned, this one doesn't solve problems, and it leaves both parties angry and frustrated with each other.

The assertive approach to communication is the one that is most desirable and leads to the best outcomes. Assertive people are able to communicate their desires and opinions in calm, peaceful, yet direct ways because they are always in control. Assertive communication never violates the rights of others. In fact, the assertive missionary can essentially call people to repentance while smiling at them. Those who are assertive in their communication listen to the responses of others, respect and value the opinions of those they have conflict with, and seek win-win solutions. That is why assertive communication is healthy—it respects both sides of the issue. In our opinion, the way the Savior would have communicated in conflicts or crises would have been assertive. He would be direct, but He would speak with love and genuineness.

In the life of a missionary, there are opportunities every day that prompt any of these responses: passive, aggressive, passive-aggressive, and assertive. However, to illustrate our point, let us share an example from the life of one missionary that recently returned from a mission in the United States.

This sister missionary related that on a particular evening, she was teaching several investigators. She and her companion realized that the only way they could manage their demanding schedule was to cancel their dinner appointment with a member of their ward. It was the only thing on their schedule that evening that was negotiable. Therefore, they called the individual and politely cancelled their dinner appointment, describing their dilemma on that particular evening. Instead of being empathetic, the member on the other end of the phone verbally blasted the missionaries, letting them know how disappointed she was in them and what poor missionaries they were for cancelling the appointment. Now, if you are a missionary, how do you respond to a ward member who tears into you like a grizzly bear? Let us consider some options.

The Passive Response: The passive approach is what the missionaries chose to take. As President Spencer W. Kimball would say, they "ate humble pie," took the brunt of the verbal tongue-lashing, apologized to the member for their transgression, and quietly hung up the phone. One of the key problems with this approach is that the member didn't learn where the missionaries were coming from and the problem certainly wasn't solved. In the phone conversation, the missionaries did nothing to explain their position or defend themselves. The angry ward member thought the missionaries were inept before the phone conversation, and the missionaries said nothing over the phone that changed her opinion. Moreover, the missionaries held much resentment toward this member, and those feelings continued to fester over time. The member didn't have kind feelings for the missionaries either.

The Aggressive Response: Though this didn't happen, the missionaries could have spoken harshly on the phone as well, accused the member of not being Christlike, rebuked her for not understanding missionary work, and hung up the phone. This response certainly isn't Christlike and it would have permanently destroyed the relationship between the missionaries and that member. Nothing good could come from this approach.

The Assertive Response: Here is what the missionaries could have done to create a win-win situation. First of all, they could have listened intently to the member's tongue-lashing. After a few moments of listening, the missionary on the phone could have said, "Sister Brown, I can see that you're really upset that we won't be able to come to dinner tonight. As you know, our charge—in fact, our mission—is to teach the gospel of Jesus Christ. We have two opportunities to do that tonight with teaching appointments. If we don't teach those lessons, who will? If you were us, what would you do?"

Sister Brown, who was aggressive in her communication, might fire back—smaller bullets this time—and asked the missionaries why they couldn't have planned better, or something of that nature. However, the assertive missionaries would seek for the win-win situation. Again, they would apologize. A more seasoned missionary might even ask, "Sister Brown, you seem upset tonight. There seems to be more here than us just cancelling a dinner appointment. Is there something we could do to help?" Who knows how Sister Brown might respond. Perhaps she would hang up or begin telling her life story. Nevertheless, the missionaries would have maintained a Christlike approach. Perhaps they could suggest meeting another night that week with less conflict in the schedule. Maybe they would consider going over to Sister Brown's home on P-day to perform some kind of service and start healing some wounded feelings.

The missionaries in this dialogue have been kind and respectful. They explained their dilemma and asked Sister Brown for a solution. If Sister Brown were to come to her senses, she would apologize to the missionaries for her rudeness and invite them over another night. However, even if Sister Brown did not come around, the missionaries have tried their best to resolve her concern, and if she refuses to accept their apology, then the problem has become hers and hers alone.

Parents, there are many role-plays and scenarios you could create to help your children work through these kinds of situations. You can coach them and teach them how to be assertive. It may not come naturally at first, but with some training, they will catch on.

The key to becoming a good communicator is learning to become more like Christ. Talk the way He does, say the things He would say. Potential missionaries should learn to speak "with the tongue of angels" (2 Nephi 32:2). They should learn to give compliments and praise freely. They should be taught how to bless, heal, and renew people through kind words and expressions. Parents must model this Christlike communication in the home.

PRACTICAL APPLICATION

- Take time on a regular basis to teach your children manners, politeness, courtesy, and people skills.
- Teach your children how to break the ice when they meet someone for the first time, or when they are invited into someone's home. Instruct them on how to ask questions that will show others they are interested in them.
- Study the talk entitled "Christlike Communication" by Elder Lionel Kendrick for a family home evening.
- Role-play scenarios in order to demonstrate passive, aggressive, passive-agressive, and assertive approaches.

SUPPLEMENTAL RESOURCES

1. L. Lionel Kendrick, "Christlike Communications," https://www.lds.org/general-conference/1988/10/christlike-communications?lang=eng.

2. Marvin J. Ashton, "Family Communications," https://www.lds.org/general-conference/1976/04/family-communications?lang=eng&query=Communication.

3. W. Craig Zwick, "What Are You Thinking?" *Ensign*, May 2014.

REFERENCES

1. L. Lionel Kendrick, "Christlike Communications," *Ensign*, November 1988.

2. Stephen R. Covey, *Marriage and Family: Gospel Insights* (Salt Lake City: Bookcraft, 1984), 198.

3. Orson F. Whitney, in Conference Report, April 1917, 43.

CHAPTER 12
MAKING YOUR HOME AN MPC

"Good homes are still the best source of good humans."[1]
—Neal A. Maxwell

NOW THAT YOUNG men and women can receive mission calls at an earlier age, missionary preparation must likewise begin earlier. Therefore, the home should become the first missionary training center our children enter. Or better yet, we should make our homes into *missionary preparation centers*. The home is the sanctuary where wise parents teach their children "faith, prayer, repentance, forgiveness, respect, love, compassion, work, and wholesome recreational activities."[2] Home is a refuge from the storms of life, the laboratory of love. It is where some of life's greatest lessons are taught, and it should be where children begin to form their testimonies and strengthen their conversion. If our homes are to become *MPCs*, the Spirit must be present in abundance, there must be wonderful friends and teachers, the gospel should be taught in purity and simplicity, and (of course) there should be great food and fun.

One of the first things that parents could do to convert their homes into *MPCs* is to create a spiritual environment or culture where the Spirit is always present—just like the MTC. In fact, there is such a wonderful environment at the MTC that many elders and sisters don't want to leave! There are numerous things that parents can do to create an environment where the Holy Ghost can dwell in their homes. If a home is guest friendly, children will feel comfortable bringing their friends there. If you are the kind of parent who doesn't want children hanging out at your home, we say to you, "Repent!" You can change. It is to your advantage to have neighborhood children hanging out and playing in your home. That way, you will at least know what is going on in your children's lives. So dust off the Xbox, pull out some board games, set up the ping-pong table, make sure the basketball hoop has a new net, and fix the trampoline in the backyard. Also make sure the refrigerator is full of food, preferably pizza and root beer. Finally, when those neighborhood kids do come over, smile and try to make them feel welcome. Treat them as you would your own children. Your kindness may one day influence some of your children's friends into becoming interested in the gospel.

One young man from the suburbs of Houston, Texas, shared the following experience:

> I, as well as several of my friends, did not grow up in the Church. While in high school, we met a young man named Alan, who was a strong, faithful, and righteous young man. We saw Alan's example every day at the school we attended together. He was the quarterback on our football team, had excellent grades, and was polite and respected by many. We were drawn to him because of the way he lived his life. In fact, we enjoyed doing social things with Alan because he showed us that we could have fun and still keep the commandments.
>
> However, it wasn't until our friendship with him deepened and we began hanging out at Alan's home that the seeds of the gospel he planted took root in our hearts. First of all, his family was especially kind to us. Within a matter of weeks, we felt that we were part of their family. We sat in their kitchen, ate their food, joked with the family, and did many fun things together. If their family was going to the lake or to a movie, the three or four of us tag-alongs were always invited.
>
> As our relationship with Alan and his family grew, we were able to see that the gospel wasn't just something they talked about; it was something they lived. Their home was filled with the Spirit. It was obvious that Alan's parents were deeply in love and that they had great relationships with all of their children. Just as apparent was how the

children all loved each other and treated one other with kindness and respect. It was just natural for gospel discussions to break out and we all enjoyed talking about the Restoration, the Atonement, marriage, modern prophets, and other gospel subjects.

Some of us began associating more with Alan's family than our own simply because we loved the Spirit we felt when we were with them. Little wonder that every one of us ended up joining the Church and are active and faithful members today. All in our group that Alan influenced served missions, married in the temple, and have served either as bishops or in bishoprics. And now, thirty years after Alan did a great job proselyting us, our children are returning from missions and marrying in the temple. We all are so grateful for the example of one young man and his great family and their home environment—they taught us how to live the happy life. Alan's parents modeled for us how we wanted our future marriages and family lives to be. We will be forever grateful!

The example of one righteous family and their home environment can influence many individuals. Besides being friendly to neighbors and our children's friends, there are other aspects of creating a spiritual environment in the home that should be mentioned. Parents can help ensure that the home is clean, orderly, and free of evil influences. Music, video games, television, computers, and other electronic media use should be monitored. When the home is a *missionary preparation center*, children can have spiritual experiences without going too far. In a gospel-centered home, there will be places to read the scriptures, to pray, and to ponder and contemplate the issues that surround us.

Creating a spiritual environment in the home isn't solely the responsibility of the parents. Children are also part of establishing such an environment. Children should contribute to the Spirit in the home by doing their chores, reading their scriptures, saying their prayers, living the gospel, eliminating contention and arguing, helping younger siblings with their needs, and myriad other things. Parents cannot do all of this alone. A family is like a successful football team, where the father is the quarterback, the mother is the running back, and the children are the offensive line and receivers. We all know what would happen if the offensive line refused to block. The quarterback would get sacked before he could even hand the ball off to the running back. If anyone on the team fails to complete their assignment, the family will fail miserably, and parents will have a high degree of frustration.

We would like to conclude our book with several ideas to help families make their home into an *MPC*. We are certain that there are other ideas that could be just as helpful. Consider how each one of these steps is modeled in missionary training centers throughout the world and find ways to incorporate these principles into your home life.

KEYS TO ESTABLISHING A MISSIONARY PREPARATION CENTER

Have a strong, positive relationship with your children

If parents do not have good relationships with their children, they will not be able to influence, teach, train, or discipline them. Parents' influence and teachings can only be as strong as the relationship they have with each child in their family. If there is no relationship, there will be no influence or teaching. That is why parents need to listen to, talk and laugh with, and be friends to their children.

Parents who have such relationships with their children will be able to influence their testimonies, help deepen their conversion, and prepare them to serve successful missions. If parents are Christlike in their demeanor, their children will gravitate to them. Most often, children come to love their parents because they know their parents love them. With love as the common bond, children are more likely to listen to the teachings of their parents and follow their counsel and way of life. *Rules without relationships almost always leads to rebellion.* On the other hand, when relationships between parents and children are strong, children are more apt to embrace the values, beliefs, and the teachings of their parents.

Family Prayer

In the Book of Mormon, we read, "Pray in your families unto the Father, always in my name, that your wives and your children may be blessed" (3 Nephi 18:21). Family prayer is not a revelatory concept; in fact, our assumption is that most people who read this book are probably having prayer with their families at least a couple times a day. Surprisingly, however, a study by Brent L. Top and Bruce A. Chadwick showed that fifty-nine percent of active Latter-day Saint families have regular and consistent family prayer, and twenty-eight percent of families rarely or never have family prayer.[3] So, even though holding family prayer is *common sense*, it is not necessarily *common practice.*

Nevertheless, understanding why we have family prayer can become a significant factor in strengthening the testimonies of our children. Henry B. Eyring taught that the "purpose of family prayer . . . must be to seek spiritual experiences for our children."[4] Therefore, when we kneel down with our families to pray, parents should seek and expect spiritual experiences rather than attempt to get the prayer over with quickly.

On in other words, we are not merely praying in our families to check a box or to go through the motions. The purpose of our family prayers is to pray for those who need help, feel the Spirit, receive answers to our problems, have comfort and guidance, and experience revelation. Moreover, children are more likely to develop the habit of personal prayer if their families have daily prayers together.

Home artwork and media that is conducive to the Spirit

Missionary training centers throughout the world are adorned with beautiful artwork and décor that invite the Holy Spirit to be present. Likewise, the spiritual environment in the home can be enhanced with gospel-related artwork such as pictures of the temple, paintings of the Savior, and other forms of art. If a new friend or acquaintance entered your home for the first time, would they know you are a Latter-day Saint?

Furthermore, it is important for children to understand what such work represents, and how parents feel about what they are displaying. Too often beautiful paintings or prints simply become part of the furniture. If children can learn the significance and meaning of the art, their testimonies can be impacted in positive ways. There should also be plenty of Church books, magazines, music, and videos to help make your home a house of God.

President Howard W. Hunter said, "Let us share with our children the spiritual feelings we have in the temple. And let us teach them more earnestly and more comfortably the things we can appropriately say. . . . Keep a picture of a temple in your home that your children may see it."[5] According to President Hunter, it's not enough to simply hang a picture on the wall; instead, we must share with our children our feelings about the temple. We can also share how we feel when we leave the temple and the strength we receive by our attendance there.

Our homes can become like temples as our children feel the peace and the Spirit that come from such tranquil surroundings. Imagine a home with gospel art, beautiful music playing with a gospel message, and a soft, safe place to relax and ponder the scriptures or other gospel principles. Children growing up in such an atmosphere would enjoy the presence of the Holy Ghost.

President Ezra Taft Benson invited all parents to "display on their walls great quotations and scenes from the Book of Mormon. . . . I have a vision of homes alerted, of classes alive, and of pulpits aflame with the spirit of Book of Mormon messages."[6] Such a home would become an *MPC* for young men and young women who are striving to become disciples of Christ.

Hold consistent family home evenings to teach the gospel

Faithful members of the Church understand the value of family home evenings. However, like family prayer, that doesn't ensure that families are engaged in regular family home evening activities. In Brent L. Top and Bruce A. Chadwick's study, they found that only forty-three percent of LDS families held FHE regularly and consistently and that thirty-eight percent of the families interviewed rarely or never held FHE.[7]

And for the families who do hold family home evening, some may treat it as an afterthought. Many parents put little time or effort into preparing powerful lessons that will impact testimonies and change lives. Instead, they end up going out for an ice cream cone after watching a younger brother's soccer game and call that good because everyone was together. Though it is wonderful for families to eat ice cream and watch sporting events, that isn't the kind of activity that our prophets had in mind when family home evening was instituted. That may be part of it, but there is much more to be desired.

President Spencer W. Kimball spoke powerfully and directly about family home evening. Listen to a prophet's pleading:

> We must not forget this home evening every Monday night. I say *every* Monday evening. We don't have other meetings, we don't go to shows, we don't go to ball games, we don't go to anything, because Monday has been set apart by the Lord and His people to hold the home evening. That is where we are going to save nations. That is where we are going to have peace on earth, and it can come only through the family as the sacred unit that can be depended upon. So we have the home evening, and there we don't just have fun, we don't

just have refreshments, and we don't just sit around and talk and play games. We have something serious in every home evening. The father is the head of every home, and even though the mother may be just as brilliant or more so, the father has been set apart by the Lord to look after his family. He can preside at that home evening and have a glorious program with all the members of the family taking part. We expect him to do it. . . .

Merely going to a show or a party together, or fishing, only half satisfies the real need, but to stay home and teach children the gospel, the scriptures, and love for each other and love their parents is most important.[8]

If parents want to create opportunities for their children to become deeply converted to the gospel, then they will hold consistent family home evenings. Furthermore, they will teach the gospel and testify of its truth. As parents share with their children how such teachings have blessed their lives, their children's testimonies will be strengthened. This doesn't mean that there can't be snacks or a fun activity afterward. We are simply suggesting that parents should not forget the most critical part of Monday night—teaching the gospel and testifying of it. A wonderful curriculum for parents and children is the new *Come, Follow Me* lesson material that can be found at https://www.lds.org/youth/learn?lang=eng. This way, Sunday School teachers and youth advisors can reinforce what parents are teaching in the home instead of the other way around.

Have regular family scripture study

Scripture study is a subject that most of us could speak about in a sacrament meeting talk and powerfully testify of its effectiveness. However, fewer and fewer LDS families are engaging in the practice. According to Brent L. Top and Bruce A. Chadwick, only twenty-nine percent of Mormon families hold regular and consistent scripture study. Fifty-two percent of the families surveyed rarely or never study the scriptures with their families.[9] That is tragic.

When it comes to family scripture study, we aren't in a competition to see how fast we can read or how soon we can complete the task. We are not reading the scriptures to check a box or meet a requirement. The purpose of scripture study is to teach our children the saving doctrines, to help them become acquainted personally with Jesus Christ and other heroes in the scriptures and feel the Spirit in their lives.

Years ago, President Henry B. Eyring declared, "We can also share scripture reading with our children in a way that makes it likely they feel spiritual assurances and can feel our acquaintance with the scriptures and the master."[10] When families immerse themselves in the scriptures, they come together in the Spirit. They treat each other with kindness and courtesy. They have greater power to resist temptation. If we want to prepare future missionaries, we must study the scriptures with them.

Hold regular parent-child interviews

Why do mission presidents interview their missionaries regularly? We are sure there are many viable reasons. However, on a basic level, we know that the interviews give the mission president—a man who may preside over two hundred or more missionaries—an opportunity to visit one-on-one. These interviews give a mission president the chance to connect with his missionaries, teach them gospel principles, and resolve any concerns or issues that may exist.

In a similar way, parents should interview their own children for the same reasons. Parent-child interviews are a wonderful way to build relationships and strengthen testimonies. Such interviews can be formal or informal. Formal interviews are useful if they occur on a *regular* and *consistent* basis. These interviews are a great opportunity for parents to bond with their children, renew their love, laugh together, catch up on events, teach, and testify. A parent-child interview also allows a father or mother to become intimately acquainted with their children, their issues and struggles, what their thoughts and beliefs are, and what they have taken interest in.

When you interview your children, find out about their classes, seminary, and Sunday School. Converse with your children about their friends, goals, and dreams. Learn about their challenges and temptations. If a parent is in tune with the Spirit, then they will ask the right questions. Connect with them by sharing your childhood memories that pertain to the children's own experiences. Such one-on-one meetings are a great way to access your son's or daughter's readiness for the mission field, and to help further prepare him or her to be ambassadors of the Savior.

Parents must set a strong example of gospel living

Parents must practice what they preach! To convert our homes into *missionary preparation centers*, parents have to set the example of Christlike living. Can you imagine what kind of bedlam we would have at a missionary training center if the mission president were quasi-active, used inappropriate language, or violated the Word of Wisdom? What about a mission president who never showed up for meetings or wasn't engaged in his calling?

In order to create a positive home environment where our children can feel the Spirit, and where their testimonies can grow, the example set by parents is critical to the process. A righteous father and saintly mother would rarely have to preach to their children; instead, their lives would be their message. Brigham Young taught parents that they should never permit themselves to do anything that they "are not willing to see [their] children do. We should set them an example that we wish them to imitate."[11] A father can't scold a son for having a temper tantrum and then get mad and throw his own briefcase across the room when he can't find his car keys. A mother can't discipline her daughter for gossiping if she is the source of all rumors in the ward. If children see their parents preaching one thing and doing another, it can kill their desire to gain a testimony.

Teenagers can smell hypocrites a mile away. Such youth often reason, "If my parents are jerks and have testimonies, what good has the gospel done for them?" Therefore, children need to see the power of the gospel in the lives of their parents. They need to see that their parents have strong faith—that they actually believe things will work out. They need to witness firsthand their parents calling on the powers of heaven during a crisis or simply living the gospel day to day. Furthermore, children need to see that their parents don't simply *believe* in Jesus Christ, but that they know Him and want to be like Him. Children need to see their parents reading the scriptures and visiting the temple often. Many parents try to live these principles behind closed doors, but it's okay for your children to catch you in the act of reading, studying, praying, and keeping the commandments.

Teach your children the power of serving others

In his address to the people, King Benjamin reminded parents of their most important duties. He said to "teach them to walk in the ways of truth and soberness; ye will teach them to love one another, and to serve one another" (Mosiah 4:15). Teaching children to serve and care for others, to be in tune to the needs of others, and to think more about others than themselves is paramount in preparing them to be rock-solid missionaries. There is no greater remedy for selfishness, no greater medication for greed, no better cure for contention, and certainly no better tonic for idleness than good old-fashioned service.

Teaching your children to be in tune to the needs of others and to help those in need is the essence of the gospel, and of missionary work for that matter. Good missionaries spend their days trying to find ways to help those around them. By serving and helping others, our children can feel the Spirit as it attends those who "succor the weak, lift up the hands which hang down, and strengthen the feeble knees" (D&C 81:5). When a self-absorbed teenager can go and visit a widow in the ward alongside his or her faithful parents, the Holy Ghost will begin to erode, layer by layer, pride, selfishness, envy, and a host of other sins. The less selfish our children become, they more apt they are to feeling the Spirit of the Lord. President Thomas S. Monson invited us to reach out to those around us. Recently, he declared, "My brothers and sisters, we are surrounded by those in need of our attention, our encouragement, our support, our comfort, our kindness—be they family members, friends, acquaintances, or strangers. We are the Lord's hands here upon the earth, with the mandate to serve and to lift His children. He is dependent upon each of us."[12]

Use family trips and vacations to teach the gospel

We are amazed how numerous families travel each summer, or perhaps even during the school year, but they have not had the opportunity to visit the Church historic sites. Perhaps they have seen the beaches in Florida, visited Disneyland, been on a cruise, or travelled internationally. Yet many of these same families have never set foot on Temple Square in Salt Lake City, pulled a handcart at Martin's Cove, walked through the streets of Nauvoo, stood in the Carthage Jail, or read their scriptures as they sat in the Sacred Grove.

Parents, if you have not taken your children to these historic, sacred places, it's not too late! There is a powerful Spirit that attends these locations, and the Church has invested millions of dollars in the sites. Our leaders recognize the powerful role that historic sites play in the lives of our youth and their families. Understanding our history and feeling a connection with people who lived during the Church's early days is a priceless experience.

A father shared the following experience regarding the power of visiting Church history sites:

After my wife and I graduated from Brigham Young University back in the mid-eighties, we packed up our car, along with our nine-month-old daughter, and headed across the fruited plain. Our destination was the Hill Cumorah Pageant where we would be participants in the cast. My wife's family had participated a few years earlier, and it was an experience that solidified their faith—especially their children. We hoped to have that same experience as a couple, and with my wife's family, who would be there.

One of our first stops along the way was Nauvoo. I fell in love with Nauvoo the minute we drove into the town. One of the more powerful experiences for me was in Carthage Jail. We arrived there at dusk on a July evening. The missionaries who conducted the tours were just closing everything up as it was time for them to go home. However, we explained that we had been driving all day from Utah and asked if there was any way for us to see the jail. Thankfully, they opened it up and gave us a great tour. Though they were only nineteen or twenty years old, these missionaries seemed to be seasoned veterans. They were mature, sincere, and excellent teachers. They bore powerful testimonies of the Prophet Joseph Smith and the Restoration. On that July evening, it was just our little family and two Mormon missionaries in Carthage Jail, and the Spirit was powerful. I will never forget it.

More than eighteen years later, our family grew from one child to eight. The little nine-month-old daughter had grown up and was now heading off to Brigham Young University to begin her college years. Our family wanted to do something special before she left. Even though funds were tight, we put our money together and planned a trip to Nauvoo. It was a great and memorable experience with our family. However, on the day we went to Carthage Jail, the circumstances were much different than they were eighteen years earlier. Instead of us being the only family at the site, there were hundreds of people. Buses were pulling into the parking lot by the dozens. Moreover, instead of the cool of a summer's evening, it was blazing hot in the middle of the day. After waiting for at least an hour, it was our turn to go into the jail with probably twenty or thirty other people. Some of the parents didn't control their children as they should have, and there was more of a feeling of irreverence rather than sacredness and peace. One baby screamed through the whole experience and several other children made tons of noise and were extremely disruptive.

As a father, I was frustrated when I walked out of the jail. All I wanted was for my children to have the same hallowed experience that I'd had years earlier, but it was not to be. When we drove home the next day, I felt a little frustrated that we had spent so much money and made such a sacrifice to come to Nauvoo (and obviously the Carthage Jail) for practically nothing. Though our children had other good experiences in Nauvoo, including the amazing pageant, I still felt a bit gypped by the experience.

However, the following Sunday, that same oldest daughter bore her testimony in the August fast and testimony meeting in our home ward. She talked about the great experience she had while in Independence, Far West, Adam-ondi-Ahman, and Nauvoo. She testified of the Spirit that she felt in those holy places, which included doing baptisms for the dead for her own ancestors in the Nauvoo Temple. However, she said the most sacred and profound experience for her was the Carthage Jail. While in there, she said she'd never felt the Spirit stronger. She felt the power of Joseph Smith's calling and she knew without a doubt that he was a prophet.

There it was—the payoff. The Lord was merciful. Despite the noise and irreverence, that daughter, as well as our other children, had one of the most sacred and profound experiences of her life up to that point. All of the sudden, the cost of the trip seemed irrelevant. I would have spent every last dime I had to take that trip, just for that one child to gain the testimony she did.

So load up the car and plan your vacation around visiting Church sites. If there is something else to do near the site, then you have a bonus. How much better would it be to visit the Orlando Temple and *perhaps* Disney World while you are in the area instead of the other way around? There is rich Church history almost everywhere. When you travel, stop at temple grounds and bask in the Spirit there. Visit other Church historical sites. Parents, share your testimony of why these hallowed places are so important to you. It will make all the difference. We would never want to imply that you have to visit sacred places in order to have a full and complete testimony, but when prospective missionaries have been to some of these sacred sites, their testimonies are enhanced and they should be able to convey—from experience—their powerful feelings about such sacred places as they teach investigators.

Apply the Wright rule

One of the most significant transitions that young men and women have to make when they enter the mission field is the structure, the rules, and the system that every missionary must live within to succeed. Many of their freedoms have been relinquished. They can't simply do whatever they want.

One of the most important lessons missionaries must learn is to always be where they are supposed to be. If there is a ward correlation meeting or an appointment with an investigator, a missionary must be there! Missionaries must also be engaged in doing what they are supposed to be doing. For example, missionaries shouldn't spend their time visiting malls, lollygagging at members' homes, or taking naps during the day. Missionaries be should intensely engaged in sharing the gospel message all day long.

In 2 Samuel 11:1, it states, "And it came to pass, after the year was expired, at the time when kings go forth to battle . . . David tarried still at Jerusalem." Not being where David was supposed to be cost him big time. As a result, he committed adultery with Bathsheba, and then had her husband, Uriah, murdered. David and his posterity suffered horrendous consequences for this choice.

Friend and colleague Dr. Randal A. Wright and his wife, Wendy, made this their family mission statement: "Be where you are supposed to be, when you are supposed to be there, doing what you are supposed to be doing." Dr. Wright then shared this insight:

> My boys are both Eagle Scouts, but I would be the first to admit that they were not very good scouts. Then how did they obtain that high rank? There is only one explanation: They were always where they were supposed to be. It was our family tradition. On Wednesday nights, they always went to their scout meetings. If there was a campout, merit badge activity, etc., they were in attendance. I have noticed if youth go to seminary every day for four years, they will graduate. If they go to high school for four years, they will graduate. I have also seen that if students go to college every day, taking a full load for four years and study, they will be college graduates. It is the same with life in general. Most success in life is showing up and sticking to the task at hand.[13]

If our children are where they are supposed to be, when they are supposed to be there, doing what they are supposed to be doing, their conversion will deepen. They will make the right choices. They will serve missions, marry in the temple, and build the kingdom of God throughout their lives.

Unfortunately, too many parents today give their children outs. If the children don't want to attend youth conference, Wednesday night activities, seminary, or even Church, parents are prone to let their children off the hook because they do not want to fight. There are peaceful solutions to such alternatives, but perhaps the best answer is to teach children the Wright family principle while they are young. Make it your family motto too. You and your children will be greatly blessed. Ten years from now, when the Saturday morning general conference session begins, your adult children will be gathered with their children, in the right place.

Teach your children how to be friendly and sociable

Many missionaries today lack basic social skills. Besides spending an inordinate amount of time with technology as children, perhaps they haven't been taught by their parents how to look others in the eye, shake hands firmly, and speak about the gospel with faith and enthusiasm. Recently, one of us attended a baptism where the missionaries were asked to speak. There were many nonmembers in attendance, and most of us expected that this would be an opportunity for the missionaries to shine. Instead, these missionaries had a difficult time communicating their messages. They spoke as if they were depressed about being missionaries, and they stared at the floor as they delivered their messages. After, when someone attempted to greet them, once again the missionaries struggled with making eye contact, had flimsy handshakes, and looked as if they really didn't want to be at the meeting. In fact, in a room mixed with members and nonmembers, the missionaries practically clung to each other, not venturing across the room to meet, greet, and socialize. They missed a golden opportunity to show what the gospel has done for them.

Parents, let's teach our children at an early age to have manners, be polite, and be social and friendly. They need to learn how to talk to adults by looking at them in the eye, shaking their hands firmly, and speaking to them with confidence. Our missionaries should radiate by their actions that the gospel of Jesus Christ is the most exciting message in the world. By their behaviors, people not of our faith should be able to detect that these ambassadors of the Savior are different than most young adults their age. These missionaries should be full of light, hope, faith, and confidence.

The list we have proposed here are just ideas. There are other things parents can do to help their children become strong missionaries. Seek the Lord's help and He will assist you. He will help you know what to focus on. He will lead you by the hand, and give you answers to your prayers (see D&C 110:12).

Parents, we have a sacred duty to help prepare our children become the greatest generation of missionaries. This cannot be done without love, sacrifice, and commitment on our part. It's not enough to merely send our children into the mission field. We owe it to them, and those they will teach, to prepare them to be the best ambassadors of the Savior our Church has to offer. They will make a difference in so many lives, and many will call them blessed!

PRACTICAL APPLICATION

- Talk about a missionary training center that you have been to. Instruct your children on what it was like. From that experience, identify ways that your home can be like a missionary training center—inside and out.
- Watch the movie "Called to Serve," produced by the Church. If you don't have access to the DVD, here is the YouTube link: http://www.youtube.com/watch?v=MaDO-Qj5kpo. Discuss as a family the role of missionaries and what they can do now to prepare for a successful mission. "Labor of Love" and "The District" can also be found on YouTube.
- As a family, invite the missionaries over for dinner or take a meal to the missionaries and thank them for the work they do.
- Have a family council meeting and discuss ways to improve family prayer, family scripture study, and family home evening.
- Have one of your children help you make a calendar where each child in the family has an opportunity to teach family home evening several times a year.

SUPPLEMENTAL MATERIALS

1. LDS website; Richard G. Scott, "For Peace at Home," https://www.lds.org/youth/video/for-peace-at-home?lang=eng.

2. LDS website; Mary N. Cook, "When You Save a Girl, You Save Generations," https://www.lds.org/youth/video/when-you-save-a-girl-you-save-generations?lang=eng.

3. LDS website; L. Tom Perry, "Protection in the Family," https://www.lds.org/youth/video/protection-in-the-family?lang=eng.

REFERENCES

1. Neal A. Maxwell, "Eternalism vs. Secularism," *Ensign*, October 1974, 71.

2. "The Family: A Proclamation to the World," *Ensign*, November 1995, 12; https://www.lds.org/topics/family-proclamation?lang=eng.

3. Brent L. Top and Bruce A. Chadwick, "A House of Faith," eds. Brent L. Top and Michael A. Goodman, *By Divine Design* (Salt Lake City: Deseret Book, 2014), 241.

4. Henry B. Eyring, "Family Followership," *Ensign*, April 1973, 29–30.

5. Howard W. Hunter, "A Temple-Motivated People," *Ensign*, February 1995, 5.

6. Ezra Taft Benson, "Flooding the Earth with the Book of Mormon," *Ensign*, November 1988, 4.

7. Brent L. Top and Bruce A. Chadwick, "A House of Faith," eds. Brent L. Top and Michael A. Goodman, *By Divine Design* (Salt Lake City: Deseret Book, 2014), 241.

8. Spencer W. Kimball, *The Teachings of Spencer W. Kimball*, ed. Edward L. Kimball (Salt Lake City: Bookcraft, 1982), 345.

9. Brent L. Top and Bruce A. Chadwick, "A House of Faith," eds. Brent L. Top and Michael A. Goodman, *By Divine Design* (Salt Lake City: Deseret Book, 2014), 241.

10. Henry B. Eyring, "Family Followership," *Ensign*, April 1973, 30–31.

11. Brigham Young, *Journal of Discourses*. 26 vols. London: Latter-day Saints' Book Depot, 1854–86, 14:192.

12. Thomas S. Monson, "What Have I Done for Someone Today?" *Ensign*, November 2009, 84–87.

13. Randal A. Wright, *25 Mistakes LDS Parents Make and How to Avoid Them* (Salt Lake City: Deseret Book, 2006), 33.

NOTES

NOTES

NOTES

NOTES

NOTES

174

NOTES

ABOUT THE AUTHORS

MARK D. OGLETREE has a MS in education and a PhD in family and human development. He taught in the Church Educational System for twenty-one years, serving as seminary instructor and principal, institute instructor, and the director of the Institute of Religion in Dallas, Texas. He has also presented marriage and family workshops in the private sector, as well as for BYU Education Week. Presently, Mark is an associate professor in the Department of Church History and Doctrine at BYU, where he teaches courses on living prophets and preparing for marriage. Mark has worked in private practice for over twenty years as a marriage and family therapist.

He has published several articles in the *Ensign*, in academic journals, and most recently teamed up with some other BYU professors and contributed to *By Divine Design*—a book on strengthening marriage and family relationships.

ABOUT THE AUTHORS

KEVIN A. HINCKLEY is a licensed professional counselor in private practice. He received his MEd in counseling at Brigham Young University, with an emphasis in organizational behavior. He has developed numerous therapeutic programs, including in-patient and day-treatment programs for addiction and trauma recovery. He has worked closely with the LDS Addiction Recovery Program and is the creator of "The Naaman Project," a day-treatment program for pornography addiction. A former bishop and institute teacher, Kevin has written five books. He is a regular presenter at Campus Education Weeks at BYU–I and BYU. He and his wife, Cindy, are the proud parents of four children and twelve grandchildren.